Acmon Pulaski Van Gieson

**Anniversary Discourse and History of the First Reformed Church of Poughkeepsie**

Acmon Pulaski Van Gieson

**Anniversary Discourse and History of the First Reformed Church of Poughkeepsie**

ISBN/EAN: 9783337296131

Printed in Europe, USA, Canada, Australia, Japan

Cover: Foto ©Lupo / pixelio.de

More available books at **www.hansebooks.com**

# ANNIVERSARY DISCOURSE

AND

# HISTORY

OF THE

# FIRST REFORMED CHURCH

OF POUGHKEEPSIE.

BY THE PASTOR,

REV. A. P. VAN GIESON, D.D.

PUBLISHED BY REQUEST OF THE CONSISTORY.
POUGHKEEPSIE.
1893.

# CONTENTS.

## TWENTY-FIFTH ANNIVERSARY.

| | PAGE. |
|---|---|
| ORDER OF SERVICES, | 7 |
| ANNIVERSARY DISCOURSE, | 13 |

## HISTORY OF THE CHURCH.

| | |
|---|---|
| ORGANIZATION, | 31 |
| INCORPORATION, | 31 |
| SEAL, | 33 |
| UNION WITH CHURCH OF FISHKILL, | 34 |
| SUCCESSION OF MINISTERS. | |
|     CORNELIUS VAN SCHIE, | 35 |
|     BENJAMIN MEYNEMA, | 46 |
|     JACOBUS VAN NIST, | 54 |
|     HENRICUS SCHOONMAKER, | 55 |
|     ISAAC RYSDYCK, | 57 |
|     STEPHEN VAN VOORHEES. | 64 |
|     SOLOMON FROELIGH, | 65 |
|     JOHN H. LIVINGSTON, | 67 |
|     ANDREW GRAY, | 69 |
|     CORNELIUS BROWER, | 71 |
|     CORNELIUS C. CUYLER, | 71 |
|     SAMUEL A. VAN VRANKEN, | 72 |
|     ALEXANDER M. MANN, | 73 |
|     GEORGE M. MCECKRON, | 75 |
|     A. P. VAN GIESON, | 76 |
| SUCCESSION OF ELDERS AND DEACONS, | 76 |
| SUNDAY SCHOOL, | 82 |

|  | PAGE. |
|---|---|
| EDIFICES FOR WORSHIP. | |
|    First Edifice, | 84 |
|    Second Edifice, | 91 |
|    Third Edifice, | 94 |
|    Fourth Edifice, | 98 |
| PARSONAGES. | |
|    First Parsonage, | 101 |
|    Second Parsonage, | 104 |
|    Third Parsonage, | 106 |
| LANGUAGE, | 107 |
| FORMATION OF SECOND CHURCH OF POUGHKEEPSIE, | 109 |
| MISCELLANEA. | |
|    Armen Kas and Armen Gelt, | 112 |
|    Palls, | 115 |
|    Subscribers for Call to Holland, | 116 |
|    First Things. | |
|       First Baptism, | 119 |
|       First Marriage, | 119 |
|       First Receipt for Salary, | 120 |
|       Seats in First Edifice, | 121 |
|       Deed Conveying First Property, | 122 |
| CHRONOLOGICAL CONSPECTUS, | 124 |
| PRESENT ORGANIZATION, | 127 |

Twenty-five years having elapsed since the installation of the Rev. A. P. Van Gieson, D.D., as pastor of the First Reformed Church of Poughkeepsie, on the morning of Sunday, October 16, 1892, services were held in the church according to the order recorded on the pages immediately following. The congregation of the Second Reformed Church of Poughkeepsie manifested their fraternal affection by omitting their own service in the morning, and uniting in worship with the congregation of the First Reformed Church. The Rev. William Bancroft Hill, the pastor of the Second Church, was in the pulpit with the pastor of the First Church, and took part in the conduct of the services.

# ORDER OF SERVICE.

## SUNDAY MORNING,

#### October 16, 1892.

Anthem, - - - - - *Te Deum.*

Invocation and Lord's Prayer.

Hymn.
    Holy, holy, holy, Lord God Almighty!

The Reading of the Law.

Responsive Reading (Congregation standing).

    Make a joyful noise unto the Lord, all ye lands.
    *Serve the Lord with gladness; come before His presence with singing.*
    Know ye that the Lord He is God; it is He that hath made us, and not we ourselves;
    *We are His people and the sheep of His pasture.*
    Enter into His gates with thanksgiving, and into His courts with praise;
    *Be thankful unto Him, and bless His name.*
    For the Lord is good; His mercy is everlasting;
    *And His truth endureth to all generations.*
    I was glad when they said unto me, Let us go into the house of the Lord.
    *Our feet shall stand within thy gates, O Jerusalem.*
    Jerusalem is builded as a city that is compact together.
    *Whither the tribes go up, the tribes of the Lord, unto the testimony of Israel, to give thanks unto the name of the Lord.*

Pray for the peace of Jerusalem; they shall prosper that love thee.
*Peace be within thy walls, and prosperity within thy palaces.*
For my brethren and companions' sakes I will now say, Peace be within thee.
*Because of the house of the Lord our God I will seek thy good.*
Behold, how good and how pleasant it is for brethren to dwell together in unity.
*By this shall all men know that ye are my disciples if ye have love one to another.*
God be merciful unto us, and bless us; and cause His face to shine upon us.
*That thy way may be known upon earth, thy saving health among all nations.*
Let the people praise thee, O God; let all the people praise thee.
*O, let the nations be glad and sing for joy.*
For thou shalt judge the people righteously, and govern the nations upon earth.

APOSTLES' CREED—(Congregation standing).

I believe in God the Father Almighty, Maker of Heaven and earth; and in Jesus Christ, His only Son, our Lord; who was conceived by the Holy Ghost; born of the Virgin Mary; suffered under Pontius Pilate; was crucified, dead, and buried; He descended into hell; the third day He rose again from the dead; He ascended into Heaven, and sitteth upon the right hand of God the Father Almighty; from thence He shall come to judge the quick and the dead.

I believe in the Holy Ghost; the Holy Catholic Church, the Communion of Saints; the forgiveness of sins; the resurrection of the body, and the life everlasting. Amen.

GLORIA PATRI.

SCRIPTURE LESSONS.

GLORIA IN EXCELSIS.

PRAYER.

HYMN—(Congregation standing).

Come, thou Almighty King!

SERMON.

PRAYER.

OFFERINGS—Offertory.
"How beautiful are the feet."

HYMN—(Congregation standing).
From all that dwell below the skies.

DOXOLOGY.

BENEDICTION.

## SUNDAY EVENING.

On Sunday evening the pews on the ground floor of the audience room were occupied by the Sunday School and the Young People's Alliance, and services were held in accordance with the following order:

ANTHEM.

INVOCATION.

HYMN.
Stand up! Stand up for Jesus!

SCRIPTURE LESSON.

PRAYER.

HYMN.
Praise Him! Praise Him! Jesus our blessed Redeemer.

ADDRESS BY MR. J. ELTING DEYO, President of the Young People's Alliance.

HYMN.
To God who claims our highest praise.

ADDRESS BY MR. CHESTER A. GEORGE, Assistant Superintendent of the Sunday School.*

---

* Milton A. Fowler Esq., the Superintendent of the Sunday School was unavoidably absent, greatly to his regret and that of the congregation.

Hymn.
> Onward, Christian Soldiers!

Address, by Rev. Philip W. Pitcher.

Hymn.
> All hail the power of Jesus' name!

Benediction.

## MONDAY AFTERNOON.

On Monday afternoon services were held as follows:

Rev. William Bancroft Hill, presiding.

Anthem.
> I will magnify thee, O Lord.

Reading of Scripture, by Rev. Wayland Spaulding.

Prayer, by Rev. C. H. Snedeker.

Reading, by Rev. Ernest Clapp,
> Of letters congratulatory from the Washington Street Methodist Episcopal Church, Rev. J. Elmendorf, D.D., Rev. Henry L. Ziegenfuss, D.D., Right Rev. Boyd Vincent, D.D., Rev. Prof. T. S. Doolittle, D.D., Rev. Prof. D. D. Demarest, D.D., Rev. Henry N. Cobb, D.D., Rev. Paul D. Van Cleef, D.D.

Addresses Congratulatory, by
> Rev. Wm. Bancroft Hill, pastor of the Second Reformed Church of Poughkeepsie.
> Rev. David J. Burrell, D.D., pastor of the Collegiate Reformed Church of New York.
> Mr. Daniel R. Thompson, member of Consistory.
> Rev. Francis B. Wheeler, D.D., pastor of the Presbyterian Church of Poughkeepsie.

Rev. James Nilan, D.D., pastor of St. Peter's Church of Poughkeepsie.

Rev. Benjamin E. Dickhout, pastor of the Reformed Church of Fishkill Village.

Rev. Charles W. Fritts, D.D., pastor of the Reformed Church of Fishkill on the Hudson.

Anthem.

Hear us, O Father.

Address, by Rev. J. G. Van Slyke, D.D., pastor of the First Reformed Church of Kingston.

Brief Response, by Rev. A. P. Van Gieson, D.D.

Solo.

My heart be ever faithful.

Benediction.

## MONDAY EVENING.

On Monday evening a reception was given by the ladies in the Lecture Room, at which a "Loving Cup" of silver was presented to the pastor. The presentation address was delivered by Rev. Denis Wortman, D.D., pastor of the Reformed Church of Saugerties, and was responded to by the pastor. The inscription on the cup is as follows:

PRESENTED TO THE

REV. A. P. VAN GIESON, D.D.,

ON THE COMPLETION OF THE

TWENTY-FIFTH YEAR OF HIS PASTORATE,

BY THE

FIRST REFORMED CHURCH OF POUGHKEEPSIE, N. Y.

Oct. 17, 1892.

# DISCOURSE.

II Cor. 4 : 5, "For we preach not ourselves, but Christ Jesus the Lord ; and ourselves your servants for Jesus' sake."

Thus does the Apostle Paul declare the substance of his preaching and the relation which he sustained to those to whom he preached.

The substance of his preaching is presented first, negatively. "We preach not ourselves." I am not seeking to make myself conspicuous, to display my own gifts, oratorical or otherwise, to win favor for myself, or to advance my own personal interests, in any way whatsoever.

Then is added, positively; "We preach Christ Jesus the Lord." All thought of self is swallowed up and lost in thought of Him. My sole aim is to make Him conspicuous, to display His beauty and majesty and saving power, to win favor for Him, and to advance the interests of His kingdom in the world.

Note that, according to the apostle's own representation, the substance of his preaching was, primarily, not doctrine, but a person. He knew that doctrine, however true and logically constructed it might be, could not save men, and that, if saved at all, they must be saved by a living Person ; even the Lord Jesus Christ, putting forth for them and upon them His own personal power, and doing for them what they were unable to do for themselves. All the doctrine that is contained in the epistles of Paul (and, as we all know, there is a great deal of it, and some of it not easy to be understood) was put there by him in order that it might be as a pedestal on which the personal Christ might be exalted, and as a glass through which the personal Christ might be viewed. That living personal Christ he adored with an adoration scarcely if at all inferior to that of the angels. Him he loved, with a love so intense that it set on fire his whole being. In and for Him he lived, and for Him he was ready, if need be, to die. Living in and for Him, he had found true life, the only life that is fit for a man to live ; and therefore he preached Him ; that living, personal Christ ; made it his whole business to tell others about Him, in order that others might be drawn to Him, and so become partakers of the same glorious and eternal life. In these letters to his Corinthian brethren he tells them, not only that he preached Christ Jesus the Lord, but also that he was determined to know nothing among them save Jesus Christ and Him crucified.

Such was the substance of his preaching. Then follows his conception of the relation sustained by him to those to whom he preached. "And ourselves your servants for Jesus' sake." The Apostle had learned that the only true nobility lies in service ; according to the word of the Master, "Whosoever will be great among you let him be your minister ; and whosoever will be chief among you let him be your servant." In learning and practising that lesson he had come into a blessed fellowship with Christ, for Christ himself took upon him the form of a servant and in order to serve sinful men humbled Himself even to the death of the cross. In learning and practising that lesson, the apostle rendered acceptable service to Christ. Elsewhere he calls himself "Servant of Jesus Christ," but he remembered, as it becomes us all to remember, that it is impossible for us to serve Christ directly. Exalted as He is at the right hand of the Majesty on high, He is above the need, and beyond the reach, of any direct service from us his creatures. The only way in which it is possible for us to render service to Him is that of indirection ; by serving men whom He loves, and for whom He died ; and, to stimulate us to such service, He has said, " Inasmuch as ye have done it unto one of the least of these, my brethren, ye have done it unto me." Therefore, the apostle served Christ by serving men. As one called to the ministry of the Gospel he served men in the highest things ; those which appertain to eternal life. To that service he devoted all his energies. In it, like his Master before him, he "emptied himself" ; through long years of self-sacrificing toil and hardship and peril, first poured out, without stint, the strength of life, and finally, beneath the headsman's axe outside the walls of Rome, poured out life itself.

Thus did the great apostle exemplify in his own person his lofty conception of the ideal minister of the Gospel. As I stand here at the close of twenty-five years of ministry among you, I feel, more deeply than any of you can feel, how far I have fallen short of that ideal. For that I humble myself before you, and still more before God.

But nevertheless, standing consciously in the presence of Him who searcheth the hearts and trieth the reins of the children of men, I can and do say with all honesty, that I have ever and earnestly striven towards that ideal ; and that, knowing that I have no sufficiency in myself, I have ever and earnestly sought sufficiency from God. You will bear me witness that I have preached not myself but Christ Jesus the Lord ; not, indeed, as the apostle did, for I have not his gifts of eloquence and inspiration ;—but to the best of the poor ability which God has given me. Christ Jesus the Lord is to me the chiefest among ten thousand and the one altogether lovely, the Son of God, the Revealer of the Father, the only and all-sufficient Saviour of sinful men, the Foundation of my most precious hope, the Source of my sweetest joy, the very Life of my life, the most glorious and most loveable Being in the whole universe ; and you will bear me witness, that, whatever else I may have failed to do, I have not failed to do my very uttermost, with God's help, to exalt Him before you, and to shew forth and magnify before you His majesty, and beauty, and atoning love, and saving power, to the end that you may be persuaded to accept, and trust, and love, and serve Him.

You will also bear me witness that I have been your servant for Jesus' sake. I have served you in love—with a love that has grown deeper and stronger with every passing year. I have served you unselfishly. Most generously have you given me of yours, but I have sought not yours, but you. I have served you with ever increasing sympathy. Your sorrows have been my sorrows, and your joys, my joys. I have endeavored to serve you not only in the pulpit and sanctuary, but also in the house and by the way. How well or ill, how efficiently or inefficiently, I have served, it becomes not me to say, or hardly even to think. The record for a quarter of a century is made up ; it cannot be made now other than what it is ; and very humbly, and with a sorrowful sense of shortcoming, I leave it with you, beseeching your charitable judgment, and with God beseeching His forgiveness for all that has been amiss.

Having spoken these few words (and these with not a little reluctance), I cease from personal reference, and pass to that which is more important. God buries his workmen, but His work goes on. Men die, but the Church lives on. On this Anniversary both Church and

Pastor are naturally brought into view, but the pastor sinks into insignificance beside the Church ; and therefore the discourse will be occupied mainly with the history of the Church, and the blessings conferred on it by its Divine Head.

Until recently the full and corporate title of the ecclesiastical body of which this Church forms a part was, "The Reformed Protestant Dutch Church in North America." This name describes briefly its character and origin. It was called *Protestant* because it protested against the errors of the Roman Catholic Church. It was called the *Reformed* Protestant Church because on certain points of doctrine, of which the chief appertained to the coporeal presence of Christ in the Lord's Supper, it differed from Luther and the Church which was called by his name. It was called the Reformed Protestant *Dutch* Church because it was founded in this country by immigrants from Holland. The first church organized by these immigrants was that in New York, then called New Amsterdam. The date of its organization was 1628. It still exists and flourishes under the name of the "Collegiate Church of New York," and is believed to be the oldest Protestant church of any denomination now in existence in this country. The fathers who founded it, true to the excellent custom of their mother country, made haste to place alongside of it a school, and this school also still exists and flourishes. It was established in 1633, five years before the organization of Harvard College. It was established as a free school and has always remained such. It was the first free school in the land and is probably the oldest educational institution of any sort whatsoever now existing in this country.

The next church founded by the Holland settlers was that of Albany, (then called Fort Orange,) which was organized in 1642. Slowly, other settlements were made in the valley of the Hudson, and at first chiefly on the western side ; and hence the next churches in order are those of Kingston, (1659) of New Paltz, (1683) and of Tappan (1694). The first church on the eastern bank of the river was that of Tarrytown, organized in 1697. At the close of the 17th Century, these last named four churches were the only churches of any denomination whatever in the whole valley of the Hudson between New York and Albany. Early in the 18th Century the tide of settlement flowed more to the eastern bank, and hence we find a church in Kinderhook, organized in 1712, and churches in Poughkeepsie, Fishkill and Claverack, all organized in the same year, 1716.

Those were the days, not only of the swamp and the forest, but also of the tomahawk and war-whoop. The " Old Van Kleeck House," which was built in 1702 on what is now Mill Street by Baltus Van Kleeck, one of the earliest settlers of Dutchess Co., and remained standing until 1835, was a fortress as well as a house, for its walls were of stone, very thick, and were pierced near the eaves and in the gables with loop-holes for musketry. And there was sufficient reason for making it a fortress, for, although this county was in fact happily free from Indian incursions, there was no certainty that such would be the case ; and the counties on the opposite side of the river suffered from such incursions, even down to the time of the Revolutionary War.

The precise date of the organization of the Church of Poughkeepsie was October 10, 1716. On that day Dominie Petrus Vas, who was then pastor of the church of Kingston, installed its first consistory, the elders being Michael Parmentier and Peter Du Bois and the deacons, Elias Van Benschoten and Peter Parmentier. The church of Fishkill was organized by the same minister and almost certainly in the same year. In 1714, only two years before the founding of these churches, the whole county of Dutchess contained only 445 inhabitants and 67 heads of families. For several years both churches were without a settled pastor, but nevertheless maintained public worship as best they could ; sometimes having the reading of a sermon by a layman, and occasionally aided by a neighboring minister who preached and administered the Holy Sacraments. Such ministerial aid, however, must, of necessity, have been of rare occurrence, for the nearest neighboring ministers were those of Kingston and New Paltz, and the records of the Church for that period show that the sacrament of baptism was administered not more than three times in any one year, more frequently only once, and in some years not at all.

In the year 1730 the two churches of Poughkeepsie and Fishkill united in calling a settled pastor for both. There was no minister in this country whom they could obtain, and they were not acquainted with any suitable minister in Holland beyond the sea. They were, however, acquainted, at least by report, with certain clergymen of high standing in Holland, in whose judgment they felt that they might repose confidence. Therefore, instead of calling some unknown person from Holland, they sent a power of attorney call to these clergymen of known standing, authorizing them to select and call some person who in their judgment would be suitable, to install him in Holland as pastor of the united churches, and then to send him to this country. This first call was made under the supervision of Rev. Vincentius Antonides, then pastor of the church of Flatbush on Long Island. It was, of course, in the Dutch language, and in that language is recorded in full on the books of this church and that of Fishkill.

This call was dated April 13, 1730, and was signed for the Church of Poughkeepsie by elders Peter Parmentier and Johannes Van Kleeck, and deacons Laurens Van Kleeck and M. Van de Bogart, and for the Church of Fishkill by elders Peter Du Boys and Abraham Buys and the deacons Abraham Brinkerhoff and Hendrick Phillips.

At the end of about fourteen months there came from the clergymen in Holland, to whom the call was addressed, an answer, stating that they had selected the Reverend, godly, and learned Herr Cornelius Van Schie, and after due examination had installed him as pastor of the united churches of Poughkeepsie and Fishkill.

Dominie Van Schie sailed from Amsterdam June 9, 1731, and arrived in New York September 9, 1731, being just three months on the voyage. On his arrival in New York he was received by Rev. Gaulterus DuBois, then one of the pastors of the Collegiate Church of New York, and was by him accompanied to Poughkeepsie. They arrived here on the evening of September 30th, went to the house of Mr. Laurens Van Kleeck, and were there met and heartily welcomed by the consistories of both churches.

Thus to their great delight the heart's desire of the people was gratified. They had a settled pastor of their own. But their delight was speedily followed by sorrow, for at the end of two years Dominie Van Schie accepted a call from the Church at Albany, and the Churches here were again pastorless; and, although they sent several earnest and even pathetic calls to Holland and Germany, they remained without a pastor for eleven years. Nor was it surprising that they called so long in vain. The country was mostly a wilderness, the settlements were few and far between, and even in the settlements the people and their dwellings were widely dispersed, the people were poor, the streams were unbridged, the roads were lonely bridle paths through silent forests. New York was then in time five times as far from Amsterdam as our missionaries in Japan are now from New York. No wonder it was not easy to find a Dutch minister, comfortably settled in Holland, who would be willing to go so far from home, and to exchange the comforts of a refined civilization for the hardships of an untamed wilderness.

But after long search the man was found in the person of Rev. Benjamin Meinema, who arrived here and became the second pastor of the United Churches in 1745, and so continued to be until 1756. After an interval of two years he was followed by Jacobus Van Nist, who was pastor for three years, from 1758 to 1761.

At this time there was raging a great controversy which convulsed our whole denomination. The parties were known respectively as the Coetus and the Conferentie. The point at issue was that of ecclesiastical independence. The church in this country was then a dependency of the Mother Church of Holland. In this country there was no ecclesiastical body higher than the consistory, which had no power of ordination. A vacant church could procure a minister only from or through Holland. If a young man born and educated in this country desired to enter the ministry, and a vacant church desired his services, the young man, however well qualified he might be, could not take charge of the church until he had first gone by slow sailing ship to Holland, and had there been ordained.

This dependency occasioned so much delay, and trouble, and expense, that to many, and especially to the younger men of the church in this country, it seemed intolerable, and they, therefore, took steps towards breaking away from it. To others, however, and especially to many of the older men, the very thought of breaking away from the mother church seemed nothing less than sacrilege. All history shows that although Dutch blood is ordinarily cool, it can get hot, and when it does get hot, it is apt to get very hot and to stay hot a long time, and such proved to be the case in this instance. The controversy was waged with fury and continued for many years. Not only the denomination, but the several congregations were divided. One part of a congregation locked the house of worship against the other part, ministers were assaulted in the pulpit, and tumults were frequent on the Lord's Day and at the church doors. The churches of Poughkeepsie and Fishkill took part in the lamentable controversy. Each congregation was divided. In 1763 one party called the Rev. Henricus Schoonmaker, a young man, who had been born, educated, and ordained in America, to be their pastor. He accepted the call and arrangements were made for his installation. The other party got possession of the church edifice, and locked the doors, and the installation service took place under an old apple tree very near the place on which the edifice in which we are now assembled stands.

The opposing party sent a call for a minister from Holland, and in response to it came Rev. Isaac Rysdyk, who, in 1765, was installed pastor of the churches, not only of Poughkeepsie and Fishkill, but also of Hopewell and New Hackensack. Thus the church was split into two contending factions, headed by two rival pastors. It was many years before the factions became reconciled, and many more years before the injury wrought by the contention was repaired.

Not far from 1774 the union between the churches of Poughkeepsie and Fishkill was dissolved, and each church sought a pastor for itself alone. The succession in this church was Rev. Stephen Van Voorhis (1773-6), Rev. Solomon Froeligh (1776-80) Rev. John H. Livingston (1781-3), Rev. Andrew Gray (1790-3), Rev. Cornelius Brouwer (1794-1807). During all these years the church was weak, and there is every reason to believe that the weakness was in a great measure the result of the bitter contentions to which reference has been made. The word of Scripture was verified that where strife is, there is confusion and every evil work. Let that sorrowful fact which stands out in the history of this church in the past be a solemn warning for all future time.

But God, in his mercy, had better things in store for this part of His heritage, and a new and brighter era dawned upon it when a call was extended to Rev. Cornelius Cuyler, and was accepted by him in the year 1808. He was installed as pastor on the 2d of January, 1809, and continued with this people until December 17th, 1833, a period of 24 years and 11½ months. This was his first charge, and to him this church probably owes more than to any other one of its long line of pastors. He, under God, was its restorer to vigor and prosperity. When he came, although there were 250 families in the congregation, there were only 43 members of the church in full communion. During his pastorate, the attendance on the church services so increased that it was necessary to tear down the old church edifice and build a new one with larger accommodations. The word of the Lord had free course and was glorified in the conversion of many. Revival followed after revival. There were two years in which the accessions to the church, mostly on confession of faith, amounted to 96 in each year. The total of accessions during the pastorate was 732, and at the end of it the church was strong, united, active, and with a membership of 462. Another grand feature of the same notable pastorate was the establishment of the Sunday

School concerning which I shall have a little more to say presently. Before taking leave of this pastorate which ended, as has been said, in 1833, I cannot help announcing that it is our privilege to have still with us, as members of the church, two of those who united with it sixty-two years ago under the faithful and successful ministry of Dr. Cuyler, and that probably they are both present with us, and participating with us in the rejoicings and thanksgivings of this day.

The next pastor was the Rev. Samuel A. Van Vranken, who remained but three years, (1834-7), at the end of which he accepted a call to the Broome Street Church in New York.

He was succeeded by Rev. Alexander M. Mann, who was pastor of the church a little more than nineteen years, (1838–57), and is still gratefully remembered by many among us. He is now the oldest living minister in our denomination, is afflicted with total blindness, but nevertheless is cheerful, alike in the remembrance of past mercies, and in the prospect of the not distant time when his eyes will be opened to behold the light that shall never fade away. The most notable event of his pastorate here was the dismission in 1850 of 27 members from this church that they might organize the Second Reformed Church of this city, between which and the mother church there has always existed the warmest affection, and the members of which have testified their affection by omitting their own service and joining with us in the service of this morning. I beg leave to say to the members of the Second Church, not only for myself but also in behalf of all my people, that we heartily appreciate and thank them for this their fraternal courtesy, and can only hope, as they also hope, that we may have opportunity to reciprocate it at the twenty-fifth anniversary of the settlement of their present pastor. If the opportunity be afforded us, we will try to improve it as graciously and as gracefully as our friends of the Second Church have improved the opportunity which has come to them to-day ; and more than that we could not hope to do, nor could they reasonably desire.

Dr. Mann was succeeded by Rev. George M. McEckron, who was installed September 7, 1858, and resigned February 18, 1867.

The present pastor began his work here on the first Sunday in October, 1867, but was not formally installed until the regular meeting of Classis which was held here on Tuesday the 15th of the same month.

The Consistory then was composed as follows :—

*Elders*—David C. Foster, Henry D. Varick, Charles M. Pelton, Daniel R. Thompson, Elvy Deyo and John R. Mathews.

*Deacons*—Charles Carman, John Van Keuren, John K. Mandeville, Lewis D. Barnes, C. S. Van Wyck and David B. Lent.

Six of these, one-half of the whole number, have since passed from the earthly service to the heavenly reward ; and every one of them has left behind him the memory of the just which is blessed. Of the remaining six, three have removed to distant churches, one has resigned on account of impaired health, and two, David C. Foster and Daniel R. Thompson, still remain in active service. David C. Foster has been in almost continuous service as deacon and elder for 50 years, and Daniel R. Thompson, for 37 years. May it please God long to spare to us their cheerful presence and wise counsel.

During the past twenty-five years, the Sunday-school has been superintended, first by John R. Mathews, and then by Milton A. Fowler, and under their efficient superintendence and the instruction of faithful teachers it has been indeed the nursery of the church.

The Young People's Alliance was formally organized December 14, 1887, and was the outgrowth from a young people's prayer meeting which was established in March, 1874, and since then has never once missed being held, whatsoever might be the weather or the season of the year.

The women, like those spoken of in the Scriptures, have laboured faithfully in the Lord, and, through their several organizations, have contributed greatly to the prosperity and usefulness of the church.

During the whole twenty-five years we have been blessed with peace and concord. There has been no dissension. Pastor and Consistory, and people and choir and sexton have wrought together in harmony.

As I look back over these years, I cannot find words to express my thanks to the members of the Consistory for their uniform kindness and efficient support.

Nor can I find words to express my thanks to you, my people, who are my joy and my crown, for all the kindness you have lavished upon me. I can only pray, as I do constantly pray, that God may abundantly reward you, by supplying all your needs according to His riches in glory by Christ Jesus.

Most of all should our thanksgiving be rendered to God, from whom cometh down every good and every perfect gift. And while we thank Him, the sense of his mercies in the past should incite us to new consecration for the present and future. May this day of gladness then be all the more glad through being one of new and glad consecration to the blessed service of the blessed Lord! O, that you who have never done it before might consecrate yourselves to Him this day, and so make it a day not only of joy to yourselves, but also of joy in the presence of the angels of God! And, O, that we who have done it before might this day consecrate ourselves to him anew, and more unreservedly; and may all the prosperity which God has bestowed in the past on this Church of his own planting be but as the first fruits of a greater harvest of prosperity which He will bestow upon it in the years which are to come; and to Him, the only wise God, Our Fathers' God, and our God, who will be our guide even unto death, and will then receive us to glory, be ascribed, as is most due, all praise, and majesty and might, and dominion, both now and forever more. Amen.

# HISTORY

OF THE

# FIRST REFORMED CHURCH

OF POUGHKEEPSIE.

TOPICALLY ARRANGED.

# HISTORY.

Under the following topical arrangement is given a History of "The Reformed Dutch Church of Poughkeepsie," popularly known as the "First Reformed Church of Poughkeepsie," more extended than time would permit in the prefixed Anniversary Discourse. Where the authorities on which the statements are made are other than those found in the records and documents in possession of the church, they are either mentioned in the text, or indicated by references at the foot of the page.

## ORGANIZATION, 1716.

The church was organized October 10, 1716. The records show that on that day Rev. Petrus Vas, who was then pastor of the church of Kingston, installed Machiel Parmentier and Pieter du Bois as elders, and Elias van Benschoten and Pieter Parmentier as deacons. Like all the Low Dutch Reformed churches then existing in this country, the church thus organized in Poughkeepsie acknowledged ecclesiastical subordination to the Classis of Amsterdam, in Holland.

## INCORPORATION, 1789.

For more than sixty years the church existed without charter or incorporation. In the minutes of Consistory for 1774 there is record of an application for a charter which is as follows, viz :

"At a meeting of the Reformed Low Dutch Church at Poughkeepsie, held at the house of Clear Everitt, the 22d day of March, A. D. 1774, it was conceived advisable to petition his Excellency William Tryon, Esq., for a charter of Incorporation of said church, etc., and for that purpose have prepared a petition, and delegated the Rev. Stephen Van Voorhees one of the Ministers, and Gilbert Livingston, one of the Elders of said congregation, to wait upon His Excellency, and present the same; and the said Consistory do hereby desire the said Minister and Elder to apply to the Consistory of the Reformed Low Dutch Congregation at New York in order to obtain their favor and assistance in the premises."

The records give no farther information concerning this petition. The presumption is that, even if it was presented, it was not granted, for there is a document which shows that the church became incorporated at a later date, under the General Act of Incorporation first passed by the Legislature of the State, April 6, 1784, and amended March 7, 1788. This document, which is still in possession of the church, reads as follows:

"We, the subscribers, being Elders and Deacons of the Reformed Protestant Church of Poughkeepsie, in Dutchess County, and being incorporated by virtue of an Act of the Legislature of the State of New York, entitled An Act making such alterations in the Act for incorporating Religious Societies as to render the same more convenient to the Reformed Protestant Dutch Congregations passed the 7th of March, 1788, and having assembled together at Poughkeepsie aforesaid on the 22d day of October in the year of our Lord 1789, pursuant to the direction of the said Act, do hereby certify unto all whome it may concern that '*The Reformed Dutch*

*Church of Poughkeepsie*' shall be, and hereby is declared to be the Name, Style, and Title by which the Trustees of the church aforesaid and their successors forever shall be called, distinguished, and known.

*In Witness* whereof we have hereunto respectively set our hands and seals at Poughkeepsie aforesaid, the seventeenth day of November, in the year of our Lord 1789.''

Sealed and delivered    HENRY HEGEMAN,      [SEAL]
   in the presence of    PETER TAPPEN,       [SEAL]
WILLIAM BAILEY,      ISAAC ROMINE,       [SEAL]
CHARLES PLATT.       JOHN FREAR,         [SEAL]
                         MYNDERT VAN KLEECK, [SEAL]
                         HENRY LIVINGSTON, JR., [SEAL]
                         ABM. FORT,           [SEAL]
                         BENJAMIN WESTERVELT, [SEAL]

On the reverse of the document is an acknowledgment signed by Zepha. Platt, and a certification of Record as follows, viz:

"Dutchess County ss. Recorded in Book No. 1 of Church Certificates, page 18 and 19, this 28th day of September, 1790.''

                       ROBERT H. LIVINGSTON.

### SEAL, 1793.

At a meeting of the Consistory held Sept. 4, 1793, under the Presidency of Rev. Andrew Gray, who was then pastor of the church, the following action was taken, viz:

" A Seal was laid before the Trustees having this device, a Star cornuted flamant, Motto, Reformed Dutch Church Poughkeepsie, (as in the annexed impression), which seal was adopted by the unamimous concurrence of said Trustees, and to be by them used, and to be distinguished by the name of the Seal of the Corporation of the Reformed Dutch Church in Poughkeepsie."

The Seal thus adopted is still in possession of the church, and is affixed to calls and other documents of importance.

## UNION OF THE CHURCHES OF POUGHKEEPSIE AND FISHKILL. 1730-1774.

The two churches of Poughkeepsie and Fishkill were organized by the same minister, Rev. Petrus Vas of Kingston, and in the same year, 1716. The congregations of both were few in number, had but slender resources, and were for several years without a pastor. In 1730 they united in calling a pastor for both, and in the call the two congregations "obliged themselves by signature that the union between Poughkeepsie and Fishkill should not be dissolved in other than an ecclesiastical manner, and under the approbation of the most Rev. Classis of Amsterdam."

The union thus formed continued a little more than forty years, and seems to have been dissolved gradually. At the time of the dissolution, each of the two churches was divided into two parties, of which one favored the Conferentie, and the other the Coetus, and each of the two parties had its own minister. The minister of the Conferentie party in both churches was Rev. Isaac Rysdyck, and as it appears from the Minutes of General Synod that he was in 1772 dismissed from his charge in Poughkeepsie, and still retained that of Fishkill, the process of dissolution may be regarded as then having begun.

The minister of the Coetus party in both churches was Rev. Henricus Schoonmaker, and as he was dismissed at

## Succession of Ministers.

a joint meeting of the two consistories held June 15th, 1774, and after that date there is no record of joint action by the consistories or churches, the dissolution may be regarded as then made complete. The approbation of the Classis of Amsterdam was not sought because the churches in this country had then become ecclesiastically independent.

### SUCCESSION OF MINISTERS.

1. CORNELIUS VAN SCHIE, 1731-3.

The first pastor of the united churches of Poughkeepsie and Fishkill was the Rev. Cornelius Van Schie, who was a native of Holland, and was born 1703. He was twenty-eight years old when he came to this country, and the churches of Poughkeepsie and Fishkill were his first pastoral charge. In defraying the expense of bringing him to America, the two churches were aided by the people of Albany ; as appears from a memorandum still existing and dated April 2, 1734, which speaks " of the money of the Albany people given to us for our Minister's coming from holand."

The call in response to which Mr. Van Schie came was addressed, not to him (for he was unknown to the churches), but to four clergymen of repute in Holland, and empowered them to select some person who, in their judgment, would be suitable, and on his acceptance of the call, to install him as pastor of the united churches and send him to this country.

The following is a translation of the call as it appears in the Dutch language on the records of both churches :

"Copy of the Power of Attorney Call to the Very Reverend Messrs. Herm. Van de Wal, Joh. Hagelis, Leonard Beels, and Tibs. Reytsma for a preacher for Poughkeepsie and the Fishkill."

As the inhabitants of this beautiful and fruitful region under God's goodness are still daily increasing in number, and in particular the descendants of those who several years since coming out one after another from Holland chose this country for their dwelling place, and avowed themselves to be members of the Low Dutch Reformed Church;

So also the congregations of Poughkeepsie and the Fishkill (lying along the North River on the east side, the southernmost part consisting of the Fishkill about twelve, and the northernmost of Poughkeepsie, sixteen Dutch miles from New York), are under God's providence so increased that they constitute a reasonable number of church members (howbeit still very few in number, particularly at the Fishkill), who on each Lord's Day attend the public worship of God under the reading of a sermon, etc., hitherto established at either village, while one and another neighboring Low Dutch Reformed minister, thereto invited by us at certain times in the year, administer the Holy Sacraments.

But earnestly desiring that we, like other congregations, may be able to enjoy the blessedness of the preaching of the Word of God and what appertains thereto by a pastor and teacher settled among us, to the end that thereby both old and young may be better advanced in the right knowledge of the pure doctrine of the gospel, that we may more regularly observe our becoming worship, and that the more zealous confirmation of the true faith in Christ with true godliness may be encouraged, &c., which, above all, is among us in the highest degree necessary, because they are so many who are as sheep having no Shepherd:

Therefore all the members of the congregations of Poughkeepsie and the Fishkill have agreed with each other to call from Holland a preacher for both congregations. Likewise they have thereto authorized us, the undersigned Elders and Deacons of Poughkeepsie and the Fishkill, for the forwarding of this pious work; and we to this end, from every one of the aforesaid members and other residents joined with us, have received a voluntary subscription for a certain sum for the making up of a sufficient yearly salary for a Low Dutch Reformed minister, according to our small ability; but in the goodness of God they are now so increasing that it seems to us that it will in a short time be much greater.

Accordingly, after taking counsel and advice from several ministers of the Low Dutch Reformed Church in this land, we, in our ecclesiastical assembly, after calling on the name of God, have resolved to convey to you, very Rev. Sirs, Herm. Van de Wal, John Hagelis, Leonard Beels and Tib Reitsima, these presents of authority for the calling of a Low Dutch Reformed minister for our congregations. We therefore also with these our presents of authority do convey to you, very Rev. Sirs, Herm. Van de Wal, John Hagelis, Leonard Beels, and Tib. Reitsima, all requisite authority, right, and power, that as wholly representing us for the Low Dutch Reformed congregations of Poughkeepsie and the Fishkill in the province of New York under the crown of Great Britain in America, you, either unanimously or by a majority of your whole number, may call an orthodox, suitable and edifying Low Dutch Reformed ordained pastor and preacher to undertake among us the preaching of the gospel. the catechetical instruction, and the administration of the Holy Sacraments according to the institution of Christ, and jointly with the officers of the Churches to exercise diligently and prudently the Church discipline, and further to do all that is required by and appertains to the office of a faithful servant of Jesus Christ, according to God's Holy Word, and the good order of the Church, after the manner of the Synod of Dort, Anno 1618 and 1619, and the custom prevailing in the Low Dutch Reformed churches in this country. And in particular, in order to a somewhat more exact definition of his service with us. the preacher who, through you, Rev. Sirs, shall thus be called for our congregations, shall, health permitting:—

1st. On each Lord's Day preach twice, and in the afternoon treat a catechetical subject according to the Heidelberg Catechism.

2nd. His Reverence shall on the first Sunday preach at Poughkeepsie, and on the next at the Fishkill, and so shall continue by turns.

N. B. The two Churches are situated about two and a half Dutch miles distant from each other.

3rd. In the winter time, from the first Sunday in November to the first Sunday in March, on account of the wide dispersion of the people and their dwellings, there shall be preaching only once on each Lord's Day ; and also, according to custom, on the first and second days of Christmas time, likewise on the New Year and Ascension Day and on Easter and Whitsunday.

4th. At least six months in the year his Reverence shall every week catechise in the neighborhood in which there was preaching on Sundays, at such time and place as may be most agreeable to him.

5th. The Lord's Supper shall be administered four times a year, equally for both congregations, to wit:—twice in Poughkeepsie and twice in the Fishkill, or oftener, as the Consistories and the preacher may deem advisable.

6th. The preparatory service is as often to be held on Thursdays before the Lord's Supper, and the Thanksgiving service in the afternoons following the mornings on which the Lord's Supper shall be administered.

7th. The pastoral visiting shall be attended to at least twice a year, once for each village, at the most suitable time decreed by the consistories.

That now you, Rev. Sirs, may seek out for our congregations such a suitable man (being a person either married or unmarried and not more than thirty-two years old) and move him to the undertaking of this service, we thus promise his Reverence:—

1st. The sum of seventy pounds, New York money, each year for the first five successive years, and then from the sixth year eighty pounds, New York money, a year.

2nd. These sums shall be paid to his Reverence during his faithful ministry among us by the Elders and Deacons, or their order, the just half to be promptly paid each half year.

3rd. The time of his salary shall begin with the lifting of the anchor of the ship on which he shall sail hither from Amsterdam.

4th. Furthermore his Reverence with his family shall also enjoy free passage.

5th. He shall reside either in Poughkeepsie or in Fishkill, or thereabout, as shall be found most fit and to his best satisfaction, and in such place both congregations shall, at the first opportunity, build for him a suitable dwelling and from time to time shall keep it in good repair.

6th. The congregation with whom he chooses to live shall furnish him sufficient firewood for summer and winter from year to year, to be piled by his house.

7th. The congregations shall at his coming present him with a suitable horse,* bridle and saddle, but afterwards, he shall provide himself with a horse for all necessary going about in his ministry among his people. Therefore shall the congregations

---

* The color of the horse bought in fulfillment of this promise is known from this receipt which is still preserved.

DUTCHESS COUNTY, September the 2th, An. Dom: 1733.

I Underwriten Hendrick Phillips own to have Received by the hands of Mr. Henry Vanderburgh, Deacon of the Reformed Prodestant Church at Poeghkeepsink, the sum of four pounds & Teen shillings In full for our half of a Certain Brown Horse Bought by the Elders & Deacons of me the Said Hendrick Phillips for the Reverend Doct. Cornelius Van Schij Minister then of Poeghkeepsink & fish Kill. I say Received pr me.

The mark HP of Hendrick Phillips.

present his Reverence from year to year three pounds additional money, three morgens of pasture, also a garden in suitable fence, and at the first opportunity shall plant an orchard with a hundred fruit trees.

8th. Also, whenever he preaches or renders any other service in that portion where he is not residing, he shall be provided with free lodging and board for the time being.

All this, we, the undersigned Elders and Deacons of Poughkeepsie and the Fishkill promise to his Reverence:—

(A.) According to the written subscription and the voluntary obligation of the members of both congregations and of other residents with us being sufficient for the full making up of the aforesaid salary.

(B.) And for the prompt fulfillment of all these we oblige and bind ourselves "qualitate qua," i. e., as present Elders and Deacons, likewise that the same shall be done by all and every one who after us from time to time shall be called to be Elders and Deacons of our congregations, and that before that they shall be installed in their respective offices, to wit, by subscribing also this instrument of calling (according to the custom usual here in several congregations in these parts,) in pursuance of the action taken by all who among us have ever been invested with the office of Elder and Deacon.

(C.) Also both congregations of one accord have obliged themselves by signature that the union between Poughkeepsie and the Fishkill shall not be dissolved in other than an ecclesiastical manner, under the superintendence of at least two ministers of the most Rev. Classis of Amsterdam, or some preachers in this land called from Amsterdam and corresponding with the most Rev. Classis of Amsterdam, and chosen thereto with the consent of both congregations, and that under approbation of the Rev. Classis of Amsterdam.

This then being our sincere intent and complete authority thus according to all the aforesaid to call a suitable and edifying minister for our congregations, we pray the Great Shepherd of the sheep, our Great God and Savior, who by His Spirit gathers His flock under the ministry of the gospel in all places and out of all people, that He may be pleased to follow these terms of our call with His blessing, to that end humbly requesting that you, very Rev. Sirs, out of consideration of the great needs of our congregations, be pleased to take the trouble to seek out and find a suitable man for our congregations, and having found him to move him to accept the ministry and to come to us at the first suitable and convenient time, seeing that a zealous servant of Jesus Christ may here win a good harvest for the extension of His Kingdom and the glorifying of His name.

Assuring him who comes to us as our pastor and teacher that we shall hold his Reverence in such esteem, love, and honor as is due to an upright minister, we shall await his coming with desire, and pray God to make prosperous ways for him. Meanwhile we will always acknowledge your good service to us with gratitude, and will pray God that He may crown with His favor and follow with His blessing your persons, ministry and families, to the magnifying of His most Holy name in the winning and saving of many souls. Amen. Signed:

FOR POUGHKEEPSIE.

| THE DEACONS. | THE ELDERS. |
|---|---|
| Laurens Van Kleeck, | Pieter Parmentier, |
| M. Van de X Bogaart, his mark. | Johannes Van Kleeck. |

FOR FISHKILL.

| Abraham Brinkerhoff, | Pieter DuBoys, |
|---|---|
| Hendrik X Phillips, his mark. | Abraham Buys. |

Further signed:

I, the undersigned, testify, as correspondent thereto invited, that this subscribing is done after calling on God's name in the ecclesiastical meeting of the Elders and Deacons of the united Churches of Poughkeepsie and the Fishkill, the 13th of April, A. D., 1730.

Vincentius Antonides,
Minister at Flatbush, &c.,
on the Long Island.

To this call there came, at the end of some fourteen months, an answer, which is also recorded in the books of both churches and is as follows:

Rev. Sirs and Brethren, constituting the Rev. Consistories of Poughkeepsie and the Fishkill:—

In pursuance of the power of attorney letters sent to us by you last year for the procuring of an intelligent and God-fearing minister for your congregations, we have proceeded to do this without delay, and thereto have chosen the Reverend, godly, and learned, Heer Cornelius Van Schie, who, in the fear of the Lord, having accepted the call, was thereupon examined with great credit at a meeting of Classis held at Amsterdam on the 4th of June, and on the same day was installed into the Holy ministry! for your congregations, and we hope that you and your congregations will find him a suitable, faithful and pious teacher and pastor who will in all respects feed the flock of God.

Wishing that the Lord may bring his Reverence to you safely with the fullness of the blessing of the gospel, and that many souls through the ministry of his Reverence may be wrested from the kingdom of Satan and joined to Christ our Lord, and that the faithful through his learned and pious instruction may grow in grace and in the knowledge of our Lord and Savior Jesus Christ; we commend his Reverence and also you all to God and the word of His grace which is able to build you up and to give you an inheritance among all them which are sanctified.

Rev. Sirs and Brothers, your well wishing Brothers,

Signed.  H. V. D. WALL,
JOHN HAGELIS,
LEONARD BEELS,
T. REYTSMA.

AMSTERDAM, June 7th, 1731.

As soon as possible after his installation, Dominie Van Schie started for his field of labor. The name of the ship on which he sailed is unknown, but from the copy of the expense account which is recorded in the church books, we learn that the Commander was Captain Laurens, and that on her voyage hither the ship stopped for a while at Dover, in England. The dates of sailing and arrival are preserved for us in a brief note made by Dominie Van Schie on the fly-leaf of the Church book of Fishkill in which he states that on the 20th of June, New Style, that is on the 9th of June, Old Style, Anno 1731, he with his wife sailed from Amsterdam, in Holland, for New York, and arrived there the 9th of September, Old Style. Hence, it appears that he was just three months on the voyage.

On his arrival in New York, he was received by the Rev. Gualterus Du Bois, then one of the pastors of the Collegiate Church of New York, and was by him accompanied to Poughkeepsie. On his arrival in Poughkeepsie, a joint session of the consistories of Poughkeepsie and Fishkill was held for the purpose of welcoming him. The proceedings of that meeting are recorded in the books of both Churches and are as follows:—

POUGHKEEPSIE, Sept. 30th, 1731.

Dominie Cornelius Van Schie having arrived here in the evening at the house of Mr. Laurens Van Kleeck, after calling on God's name, consistory meeting was held with all the consistory members of Poughkeepsie and the Fishkill; when

1st. For this occasion Dominie G. Du Bois, who, at the request of the committee of the consistory of Poughkeepsie and the Fishkill, accompanied Mynheer Van Schie to introduce him to his congregations, was unanimously requested to preside over this meeting.

2nd. Thereupon was read in consistory the letter from the authorized preachers of Amsterdam, informing them that in pursuance of their power of attorney call they had called Dominie Cornelius Van Schie for preacher of Poughkeepsie and the Fishkill; likewise the letter of the Classis of Amsterdam concerning the ordination of the same and his installation for their congregations. Whereupon Dominie Gualterus Du Bois proposed to all the members of consistory present, whether they did not, in pursuance of these letters, acknowledge this Dominie Cornelius Van Schie for their lawful ordained pastor and teacher of Poughkeepsie and the Fishkill. Hereupon they all with hearty testimonies of gladness, testified to Dominie Cornelius Van Schie with outreaching of the hands that they acknowledge and in truth shall hold him as their lawful pastor and teacher; and Dominie Du Bois wished them all health and peace and prosperity with his Reverence, &c., &c.

3rd. Thereon resolved that the letter of the Sirs H. Van De Wall, J. Hagelis, L. Beels and T. Reytsma dated at Amsterdam, June 7th, 1731, shall be copied in the church books both of Poughkeepsie and the Fishkill; as also,

4th. That the power of attorney call on Dominic Van Schie shall also be inscribed in both church books, word for word, with some blank leaves, that the same may be subscribed from year to year by the Elders and Deacons elect, as was resolved by the consistory, and as the power of attorney itself indicates.

5th. That those who may be married, baptized, and received as church members at Poughkeepsie, shall be recorded in the church book there, and so also all of this kind that takes place at the Fishkill shall be recorded in the church book of Fishkill.

6th. Also unanimously resolved that the consistories of Poughkeepsie and the Fishkill shall be and remain two separate consistories, and that each shall hold separate meetings for choosing new members of consistory and all other business which pertains to the welfare of either congregation in particular.

7th. That their preacher in joint meeting of consistory, in case of any voting on any matter coming up, as president shall have a double vote.

8th. Resolved, unanimously, by vote of the consistories of Poughkeepsie and the Fishkill, that the time of choosing the new consistories shall be at Poughkeepsie and the Fishkill the first or second Sunday in the New Year after the preaching service of the day where the preacher shall then have preached.

9th. In both the congregations and the Churches of Poughkeepsie and the Fishkill, at the first opportunity, notice shall be given to the congregations, that, in pursuance of a unanimous resolution of both the consistories of Poughkeepsie and the Fishkill, the parents henceforth shall please to present their children for baptism, only after they shall have betimes given to the pastor for record the names of the child, the parents, and the witnesses; but in case Reformed Church members come from a distance, and do not belong to the congregation under the preaching, they shall announce such (names) to an Elder present, or, if no Elder be present, to a Deacon, and then the child, if legitimate, shall be baptized, provided they promise that they will give the same, for record by the preacher, immediately after church time.

10th. With respect to the Lord's Supper, the division is thus arranged,—

(1.) In the month of October the Lord's Supper shall always be administered at Poughkeepsie.
(2.) In the month of December at the Fishkill.
(3.) On Easter or the following Sunday at Poughkeepsie.
(4.) On Whitsunday or the following week at Fishkill.
(5.) In the month of June at Poughkeepsie.
(6.) In the month of August at the Fishkill.

Subscribed. All this done in my presence,

G. Du Bois.

At the same meeting or soon afterward, Dominie Van Schie must have called attention to the expense which he had incurred on his journey. The account of such expense is recorded in both church books and is as follows:

|   |   | £ | s. | d. |
|---|---|---|---|---|
| 1. | To the Classis of Amsterdam and the authorized Sirs preachers............................ | 12 | 10 | 0 |
| 2. | Expenses from Delft to Amsterdam........... | 1 | 10 | 0 |
| 3. | 30 days in Amsterdam, making ready myself and wife and waiting for a ship to go,—each day spent 13 shillings and 4 pence............... | 20 | 00 | 0 |
| 4. | Cost of bringing my goods on board and the Custom House............................ | 1 | 00 | 0 |
| 5. | Spent at Dover............................. | 4 | 00 | 0 |
|   |   | £39 | 00 | 0 |
|   | To Captain Laurens paid for the passage of Dominie Van Schie and his wife............ | 32 | 00 | 0 |
|   | To the same Captain for fresh provision, laid in in England to eat on the voyage............ | 2 | 19 | 6 |
|   | To the passage from New York to Poughkeepsie for the preacher and his company........... | 2 | 19 | 0 |
|   |   | £76 | 18 | 6 |

Our forefathers, with their Dutch honesty, were not willing that such an account should remain long unsettled, and therefore, only four days later, another joint meeting of the consistories was held for the purpose of settling it, and also of attending to other matters pertaining to the comfort of the new pastor. The record of that meeting is as follows:

POUGHKEEPSIE, Oct. 4th, 1731.

1st. After calling on God's name, consistory meeting is again held with the consistories of Poughkeepsie and the Fishkill, and then all the articles made in the previous meeting of the 30th of September last are confirmed.

2nd. Thereon the reckoning of expense incurred in the coming over of the Heer Van Schie with his wife is taken up and was fully acquiesced in, with unanimous resolution that the same be copied in both the church books of Poughkeepsie and the Fishkill, with written approval signed by both consistories.

3rd. In order that Dominine Van Schie may have perfect freedom in choosing the place most agreeable to him at Poughkeepsie and the Fishkill, all the consistories have declared that, whenever Dominie Van Schie makes his choice, they with perfect content shall consent to the same and shall fully acquiesce therein.

4th. Whenever Dominie Van Schie shall have chosen to reside at Poughkeepsie or at the Fishkill, there where he chooses to live, both congregations together (each bearing the half of the expense) shall buy six acres, build a house, and make a garden, and plant an orchard, in accordance with the stipulations on these points contained in the power of attorney call.

5th. In case it may come to pass at any time after both the congregations of Poughkeepsie and the Fishkill shall together have bought six acres at the place where Dominie Van Schie shall have chosen to reside, and there shall have built a house and made a garden and planted an orchard, that the two congregations shall ecclesiastically separate from each other, that each may have a preacher for itself, then shall the six acres, house, garden and orchard be appraised by four impartial men, (and the said four shall have power to choose a fifth) and the congregation at the place where the preacher shall have resided shall honestly give the just half of the sum for which all the aforesaid was appraised to the congregation in which no preacher's house was built with the coming of Dominie Van Schie. Subscribed.

All this was done at the place and times aforenamed in the presence of Dominie G. Du Bois, as we, the undersigned testify.

PIETER PARMENTIER,
PIETER DU BOYS,
JOHANNES VAN KLEECK.
ABRAHAM BOYS,

CORNELIUS VAN SCHIE.
LAURENS VAN KLEECK,
ABRAHAM BRINKERHOFF,
HENDRIK X PHILLIPS,
HIS
MARK.

MYNDERT X VAN DE BOGAART.
HIS
MARK.

The duration of Dominie Van Schie's pastorate was less than two years. In 1733 he removed to Albany and took charge of the church there in acceptance of a call dated May 11, 1733.

He served the church of Albany as the colleague of Dominie Van Driessen until the death of the latter in 1738, and then as sole pastor of the church until his own death, which occurred August 15, 1744. He was buried under the church at Albany.

His last sermon was from the text, Rev. 2 : 10, "Be thou faithful unto death and I will give thee a crown of life."*

2. BENJAMIN MEYNEMA, 1745–56.

After the departure of Mr. Van Schie the united churches promptly took steps towards securing a new pastor, and to this end sent a second call to Holland. This was countersigned by Rev. George Wilhelmus Mancius, then pastor of the church of Kingston. Like the first it was a power of attorney call, directed to certain clergymen in Holland and empowering them to select and send a minister for the two churches here.

The clergymen named are three of the four named in the previous call, viz: Messrs. Hagelis, Beels and Reytsma. The name of the fourth is omitted and it is possible that he had died in the intervening time.

In its general tenor this second call resembled the first; but there are a few points of difference.

The salary offered is eighty pounds instead of seventy. Forty pounds are sent with the call to pay the passage of the minister. Now a parsonage is built at Poughkeepsie, and it is described as "a new and suitable dwelling house for the free residence of the preacher for the time being; forty-five feet long and twenty-seven broad, having three rooms and also a study upstairs, a large cellar under the house, a well with good water, a garden and an orchard planted with a hundred fruit trees." It is also stated that in case any dispute should arise between the preacher and the consistories, one or more orthodox ministers of these provinces should be selected as referees, and to their decision, subject to the approval

---

* Historical Discourse on the Reformed Protestant Dutch Church of Albany, by Rev. E. P. Rogers, D.D., 1857. Also Circular by the Consistory of the same church.

## Succession of Ministers.

47

of the most Rev. Classis of Amsterdam, the matter or matters should be wholly referred.

To this call no response came so far as is known. Certainly no response came in the shape of a living pastor. Therefore, after a time of patient waiting, the consistories sent a letter to one of the clergymen in Holland, (Rev. L. Beels) jogging his memory, and offering additional inducements. They agree to increase the salary from eighty to one hundred pounds, and say that this is more than is received by many preachers in these parts. They state that the two churches are only three hours distance from each other, and that in his journeyings from one to the other, his Reverence shall seldom be without company. They also speak of the harmony prevailing among the people, and praise God that no division of sentiment worthy of mention is to be found among them. This letter as copied in the church book, bears no date.

Time passed on. No response came and the churches were still pastorless. Having failed to obtain a pastor from Holland, the churches turned their eyes to Germany, and sent a power of attorney call to some clergymen there, urging them to seek and send a pastor, and stipulating that if the person selected were not able to preach in the Low Dutch language, he should undertake to preach in it, in one year, if practicable. This call also, as copied in the church book, bears no date. Like that which had been sent to Holland it was unsuccessful.

Failing abroad, the Church of Fishkill, weary with the long waiting, looked for a pastor nearer home. They had heard of a young man named John Caspar Fryenmoet who had been somewhat irregularly ordained and was engaged in the work of the ministry in Port Jervis and the neighboring churches on the Delaware. On the 20th of September, 1742 (at least eight years after the departure of Dominie Van Schie), the Church of Fishkill by itself, and without the co-operation of the Church of Poughkeepsie, sent a call to him, offering him eighty pounds a year and stipulating that his ordination should be made regular. But the call was not accepted.

Thus unsuccessful in this country, the churches again looked to Holland and sent another power of attorney thither. The previous call had been directed to three clergymen. This was directed to one clergyman and three laymen, namely, the Very Rev. Theodorus Van Schelluyne, and the highly esteemed Messrs. Pedro de Wolff, L. Clarkson and J. Stockers. This call is dated Poughkeepsie, January 22nd, 1744, and is countersigned by J. M. Weiss, minister of the High and Low Dutch Reformed Congregations of Rynbeck, in Dutchess County. The terms are substantially the same as those of the preceding calls with the exception that the salary is increased to the munificent sum of one hundred and ten pounds, but is to be paid yearly instead of half yearly.

More than a year passed before the answer came; but when it came it made glad those whose hearts were sick with hope long deferred, for it informed them that the authorized gentlemen had conferred the call on Dominie Benjamin Meynema, then ministering the Holy Gospel at Oudwolde and Westergeeft in the Classis of Dokkum, in Holland, and that the same had been accepted by him.

Mr. Meynema (thus he uniformly writes his name, but it also occurs as Meinema and Meenema) was born in Holland in 1705,* and is said to have been licensed in 1727. The call accepted by him is not copied in the church book of Poughkeepsie, but is recorded in full in the church book of Fishkill, and beneath it are the following (in Dutch), which are interesting as showing the

---

* See inscription on his tombstone, page 53.

formalities which were then requisite for the obtaining of a minister.

First appears this action of the gentlemen to whom the call was addressed:

"By authority of the above Power of Attorney, we, the undersigned, have conferred the call to the Congregation of Poughkeepsie and Fishkill on Do. Benjamin Meynema, at present ministering the Holy Gospel at Oudwolde and Westergeeft, on such conditions as are contained in the aforesaid instrument of Power of Attorney, who, also, on the same conditions has accepted the call.

Amsterdam, May 4, 1745.

THEODORUS VAN SCHELLUYNE,
PEDRO DE WOLFF,
LEV. CLARKSON,
J. STOKKERS,
BENJAMIN MEYNEMA.

"This signed in our presence.

THOMAS VAN BISSELIK,
CORNELIUS JANSE,
OTTO VAN DAM, (Notary public.)

Accords, so far as concerns this extract, with the original as above signed.

Amsterdam, June 9, 1745.

OTTO VAN DAM,
Notary public."

Then follows the approval of the Classis of Amsterdam to which the churches of Poughkeepsie and Fishkill were subordinate.

"The very Reverend Classis of Amsterdam, having seen and considered the call to the ministry of the churches of Poughkeepsie and Fishkill presented by the committee to the person of Benjamin Meynema, has unanimously approved the same, and hereby approves the same, with congratulations and prayers for all blessings on him who is called and on his congregation.

Amsterdam, June 14, 1745.

In the name of Classis,

JOHANNES VAN DER VORM,
Preacher at Amsterdam,
Clerk of Classis,
pro tem."

And finally appears the action of the Classis of Dokkum to which the Rev. Mr. Meynema was subordinate.

"The Reverend Classis of Dokkum, having examined the accompanying call to Do. B. Meynema, and also the accompanying approval of the Classis of Amsterdam, and thereupon having learned from the members of the consistory of the former congregations of his Reverence that his Reverence would also be dismissed by them, accordingly the Rev. Classis of Dokkum dismisses the aforesaid Do. Meynema from his charge at Oudwolde, etc.,' and assigns him to the Congregations of Poughkeepsie and Fishkill, with wishes for the precious blessings of the Lord on his person, ministry, and the congregations.

July 5, 1745.

H. REITZEMA, President of Classis Pro tem.
A. KNOCK, Clerk of Classis Pro tem."

We know not when this second pastor sailed from Holland, or when he arrived in this country; but we learn from the records of the Church of Fishkill that he was present at a joint meeting of the two consistories held in Poughkeepsie, December 22, 1745, and there presented two requests. One was that the expense incurred in his journey to this country should be paid by the congregations, and the other, that his salary should be paid half yearly instead of yearly as promised in the call. The first was promptly granted and the second, unanimously refused. The consistories would fulfill their promise to the last iota, but would not go beyond. From the record of another consistory meeting held May 18th, 1747, we learn that "the president was pleased to inquire whether he and his horse ought not to be provided with meat and drink and fodder while he was engaged in pastoral visiting"—whereupon it was "Resolved, that the consistory who go around with him shall ask and demand these for his Reverence. Also, his request that he might be reimbursed for any expense in riding to the church, or from the church to his home, on account of storm, high water, and necessity of being helped through the creek, is answered in the affirmative, since the call assigns that to him."

These extracts from the early records are interesting as furnishing a contemporaneous picture of the times. They show how much farther, in time, America was from Europe then than it is now. Then the voyage required three months of discomfort, now it can be accomplished in six or eight days of luxury. New York was then, in time, five times as far from Amsterdam as our missionaries in Japan are now from New York. They show the state of the country here—the wilderness dotted with but few settlements, and even in the settlements the people and their dwellings widely dispersed ;—the roads which were not roads, but only bridle paths, winding through the forest and so lonely that it is mentioned as a special inducement that the preacher will seldom have occasion to journey from one Church to the other without company ;—the unbridged streams for the crossing of which assistance was necessary in case of high water.

They show the condition of the Churches as to externals,—how few were the members, and how slender their resources, so that Poughkeepsie and Fishkill had to unite because neither one was able to support a pastor by itself, and even then were constrained to seek assistance from " the people of Albany."

But they show, also, the spirit of the people :—their courageous hopefulness which makes them confident that their numbers and their resources will increase ;— their true Dutch persistency, in which they seek for a pastor first in Holland, and then in Germany, and then in America, and then in Holland again, and keep on seeking through more than eleven long years until the pastor is found ;—their carefulness, in which they define just what they expect from their pastor, and what he may expect in return;—their great regard for him, manifested by hands outstretched in welcome;—their sturdy independence, for, much as they respect their pastor, he is to be no lord over God's heritage, and on occasion they can unanimously refuse his request. Above all do we see their love for the Church and its ordinances and the word of the gospel, which constrains them to pray, and strive, and tax themselves to the utmost of their ability in order that they and their children may enjoy the preaching of the word and the administration of the ordinances by a pastor settled among them.

Dominie Meynema remained pastor of the united Churches until December 23d, 1756. There is still preserved among the papers of the Church of Fishkill the paper on which, at that date, he acknowledges the receipt of three hundred and ten pounds in full of all demands, and therewith declares his voluntary resignation of Poughkeepsie and Fishkill. The paper is signed "Benjamin Meynema, gemitteerd predikant," which, being interpreted, is "Benjamin Meynema, dismissed preacher."

It would seem that his relations were not altogether amicable, either with his churches, or with the Coetus. In the minutes of the Coetus for November, 1749, there is intimation of dispute between himself and his consistories which had been referred to the Coetus for settlement. From the minutes of the same body for September, 1754, it appears that the dispute still continued, and a committee was appointed "to bring the congregation and the Dominie to peace and love and harmony for their common welfare, and in case Dom. Meinema should refuse (which may God forbid) to appear before the committee, and thus contemn it, then the committee is authorized to inquire into the charges against him, and to deal with him ecclesiastically according to the circumstances, even to his suspension from the ministerial office."*

There is every reason for supposing that the charges thus spoken of were not of any immorality, but of unamiable and dictatorial disposition and manner. The Rev. Mr. Fryenmoet, in a letter to the Classis of Amsterdam, says that the rupture between Dominie Meynema and his congregations was caused by his lack of "lovable and friendly conversations and intercourse with people," and that the quarrels and dissensions between him and them " rose so high that, finally, for the sum of three hundred pounds of our money, Dr. Meynema was compelled to desist from his services among them."

Little is known of the history of Dominie Meynema subsequent to his resignation of his charge. He was buried in the church-yard of Fishkill and on his tombstone is the following inscription:

Hier Leyde het Lighaam<br>
van De Eerwaarde Heer<br>
BENJAMIN MEENEMA.<br>
in zyn Leenens Teje predikant van de<br>
Viskels & Poughkeepsie, in de<br>
Heere Outslaapen den 9 September, 1761.<br>
Oude Synde 56 Jaar.†

His wife was Catrina Rapelye, and the inscription on her tombstone in the same church-yard states that she died January 17, 1759, aged 28 years and 6 months.

---

\* Minutes, Gen. Synod, Vol. I., pp. xli., xciii.

† Here lies the body of the Reverend Benjamin Meenema, in his life time preacher of Fishkill and Poughkeepsie. Fell asleep in the Lord, September 9, 1761, aged 56 years.

## 3. JACOBUS VAN NIST, 1758-61.

The third pastor of the united churches was Jacobus Van Nist (also written Van Nest and Van Neste), who was born in this country in 1735. The call extended to him was dated Nov. 28, 1758, and countersigned by Rev. Jacobus Rutser Hardenburg, of Raritan. It states that he was then a candidate for the ministry, and stipulates that he shall allow himself to be examined for licensure and ordained by the assembly of ministers and elders known by the name of the Reverend Coetus of New York and New Jersey. The controversy between the Coetus and Conferentie parties had then begun, and the Conferentie at its meeting in October, 1758, sent a complaint to the Classis of Amsterdam that "they (the Coetus) proceeded in the Spring to make a candidate of one Hardenburg, and afterwards, even last week, made him the minister of Raritan, and further two candidates, one Van Nest and one Barcalo."*

Mr. Van Nest was only twenty-three years old when he became pastor. His ministry was of brief duration, as in little less than two years and a half it was terminated by his death. He was buried under the pulpit of the old church of Fishkill, and the stone erected to his memory stands at present against the rear wall of the church of Fishkill, and bears the following inscription:

Hier Leydt Het Lighaam van
JACOBUS VAN NESTE, Bedienaar Des
Heylige Evangelium of Pockkeepsie
En de Viskill, In Dutchess County.
Zynde In de Heere Gereest de 10
April, 1761. Oudt Zynde 26 Jaar,
2 maande en 3 Daage. †

---

\* Minutes Gen. Synod, Vol, I, p. cii.

† Here lies the body of Jacobus Van Neste, Minister of the Holy Gospel in Poughkeepsie and the Fishkill, in Dutchess County. Rested in the Lord April 10, 1761. Aged 26 years, 2 months and 3 days.

## 4. Henricus Schoonmaker, 1763–74.

The fourth pastor of the united churches was the Rev. Henricus Schoonmaker who was born in Rochester, Ulster Co., July 18, 1739, and studied under Rev. J. H. Goetschius. The call extended to him is dated Poughkeepsie, Dec. 11, 1763, countersigned by Johannes Mauritius Goetschius, minister of New Paltz and Shawangunk, and attested on behalf of the Coetus by Rev. J. M. Van Harlingen. It is addressed to him as a candidate for the ministry and stipulates that he shall be examined, licensed, and ordained by the Coetus. The controversy between the Coetus and Conferentie was then at the climax of its vehemence, and the portion of the congregation that favored the Conferentie was bitterly opposed to the settlement of Mr. Schoonmaker as their pastor, and, succeeding in obtaining possession of the church edifice, barred the doors against the committee appointed by the Coetus for the ordination. The committee thereupon had a wagon placed under a large tree in front of the church, and the ordination sermon was preached by Rev. John H. Goetschius, standing in the wagon, and on bended knees in the wagon the candidate received the laying on of hands. A young man, John H. Livingston by name, was present and, deeply interested in the whole scene, said to one of the elders, "Thank God, though the opponents have succeeded in excluding him from the church, they have not succeeded in preventing his ordination."

Elder Peter Van Kleeck and Deacon John Conklin, of Poughkeepsie, had not signed the call, and at the meeting of the Conferentie held June 20, 1764, they appeared before the assembly with a complaint against the ruling consistory of the congregation for "making a call upon one Schoonmaker" without recognizing them in their official character, and for allowing him to preach although he had not been regularly ordained.

On the ground of these complaints it was requested that a minister should be sent to appoint a consistory according to the constitution of the church. After "a consciencious consideration of the case the request was granted," and in their letter to the Classis of Amsterdam, prepared at the same meeting, the Conferentie states "that the congregation of Poughkeepsie is under the tyranny of some consistorial persons, who were picked out of the congregation by the Coetus ministers, to serve the ends of the Coetus, by unlawfully thrusting (ten to one in the congregation being opposed), upon Poughkeepsie and Fishkill that Schoonmaker, whom they last autumn made a candidate, and have now made a minister. We have now permitted the petitioners to choose a consistory, which will serve, not only to hinder, in his disorderly course, this young man, ordained against the will of the Classis, (as they very well knew), but also to put the congregation in a condition to unite with some other settlements near by in calling a lawfully ordained minister from this country or Holland."\*

Mr. Schoonmaker was pastor of the Churches until June 15, 1774, when, at a joint meeting of the two consistories, held at Fishkill, he was dismissed, in order that he might take charge of the Church in Aquackanonck, N. J. The consistories, in giving him his dismission, testify to his faithfulness, and declare that "they had wished, if it had seemed good in the providence of God, that they might have been able still longer to rejoice in his light, and to profit by his useful and acceptable ministry."

---

\* Minutes general Synod, Vol. I., pp. cxiii–cxv.

It is said that Mr. Schoonmaker was in his time the most eloquent preacher in the Dutch language in this country. He could not preach well in English, and left Poughkeepsie and Fishkill for Aquackanonck largely because, in the former places, the use of the Dutch language was declining, and in the latter place was still maintained.

In 1816, on account of the infirmities of age, he resigned his pastoral charge, and, in the same year, removed to Jamaica, Long Island, to reside with his son, Rev. Jacob Schoonmaker, pastor of the Reformed Dutch Church in that place. There he died, January 19, 1820, in the eighty-first year of his age. His body was removed to Aquackanonck for burial among the people of his last charge, and the funeral sermon was preached by his successor, Rev. P. D. Froeligh, from the text, Zech. 1: 5.*

5. ISAAC RYSDYCK, 1765–72.

It has already been said that some in the united congregations favored the Conferentie party, and consequently were opposed to the settlement of Mr. Schoonmaker. They regarded his ordination as unlawful and invalid, because it had not been conducted by the authority of the Classis of Amsterdam. These disaffected members of the two congregations chose consistories of their own, in opposition to the other two consistories, and the consistories thus chosen sent a call to the Classis of Amsterdam, requesting the Classis to send to the churches a minister from Holland. The call was accompanied by a letter to the Classis from the Rev. John C. Fryenmoet, who was a member of the Conferentie, and was, at that time, the pastor of the churches of Kinder-

---

* Corwin's Manual of the Reformed Church, and Rev. Cornelius D. Westbrook, D.D., in Sprague's Annals, Art. Schoonmaker, Henricus.

hook, Claverack, and Livingston Manor. This letter so accurately describes the condition of the churches at that transition period, and so vividly depicts the difficulties and perplexities which were inherent in the circumstances in which they were placed, that, with the exception of a few unimportant sentences, it is here given entire :*

*Very Reverend Fathers and Brothers in Christ, composing the Classis of Amsterdam.*

In the name, and by the order, of the Rev. Consistories of the four combined congregations, Po'keepsie, Viskil, New Hackinsack, and Hoopwell, I have the honor to convey to your Reverences the enclosed letter; with their humble request that you will please to supply them as soon as possible, with an orthodox, learned, and pious minister, who shall faithfully and constantly maintain the good order of the church, according to divine and human law, regard your Reverences as a high assembly, and therefore, with us, subordinate himself to you, adhering with us to your Reverences in brotherly love, steadily and faithfully; so that by such a man, with the supporting assistance and blessing of God, the decaying condition of these calling congregations may again be restored, that the truth of our sound confession of faith, and our pure discipline, according to our laudable church rules, be protected and defended against so many interrupting errors in doctrine and discipline, which flood the church, not only with all kinds of erroneous spirits from outside, but also with promoters of the present Coetus from inside.

I consider it expedient to lay, in this letter, before your Reverences, a faithful report of the present condition of these congregations; so that you may not only perceive by it the necessity and important occasion of this call, but also be in a condition to send an able man for these congregations.

Po'keepsie and Viskil are two large congregations, from which the two others, Hackinsack and Hoopwell, have started. With consent and approval of the Consistories of Viskil and Po'keepsie they were organized as separate congregations; but the growth of the two large congregations was much retarded

---

* This letter is part of the Amsterdam correspondence belonging to the General Synod. The attention of the writer was kindly called to it by the translator, Berthold Fernow, Esq., of Albany.

by the grievous quarrels and dissensions arising between their pastor, Dr. B. Meinema, and the Consistory and congregations of Po'keepsie, and, later also, of Viskil ; which rose so high that, finally, for the sum of 300 pounds of our money, Dr. Meinema was compelled to desist from his services among them, and make thereby an opening for the call of a poorly educated Coetus youth, named Jacobus van Nist. But the breach among them was not thereby healed. It became only greater, because, during his service, which was cut short by an early death, the Consistories of both congregations wholly surrendered to the present Coetus ; that is, they withdrew from the jurisdiction of your Reverences, bragging and boasting that now they were delivered from the Papal yoke of subordination to the Classis ; (for such and much worse is their constant foul language), that they have as good a right to examine and promote as the Classis ; and that therefore it could not be suffered that other persons should ever come among them, for the ecclesiastical service, than such as were fully subordinate to the present Coetus, nor that others should be allowed to preach in their churches than Coetus preachers. For this reason, and for want of members, their number in each congregation is very small ; not more than the Consistory with very few adherents. The same men are yearly re-elected into the Consistory, and I have been forbidden the Church at Po'keepsie, because I am not a preacher of the Coetus. All this not only embitters the congregation against their Consistories, and still more against the Coetus, but also grieves and distresses them about how to extricate themselves from such a miserable condition, wherein they were without the service of the word and the seals of the covenant, except by Coetus preachers, with whom the congregations would have nothing to do.

Therefore they finally addressed themselves to me to take the service now and then among them, which I have accepted ; first in the congregations of New Hackinsack and Hoopwell, which were more peaceful, because their Consistories did not belong to the Coetus ; and then at Viskil, but there with consent of the Consistory. I have now served these congregations for 3 or 4 years, although I live between 70 and 80 miles from them. During this time I have used all possible care and trouble to reconcile the dissenting parties, and to have them call an orthodox pastor, subordinate to your Reverences ; but it was all in vain, because the Consistory of Viskil obstinately stood to their resolution not to have anything further to do with the Classis or Synod, but only with the Coetus, and therefore to call, contrary to the will and wish of the Congregation, a young man who was to be examined and promoted against the express prohibition of the Classis and Synod.

Then the congregations of New Hackensack, Hoopwell, Kloof, with the subordinate one of Viskil Ferry, resolved to send a call to Dr. Blaeuw, Minister at the Gansegat; and it was done in the presence of myself as adviser. As, however, he raised difficulties about accepting the call, because not the Consistory of Viskil, but only the deputies of the congregations had signed it, the subordinate members of this congregation urgently requested me to help them to a Consistory, that their call might be made complete, because their Coetus Consistory would not do it. At first I found many difficulties; but after consulting with my Consistory, and after examining and considering, with six of my elders, the condition of the Viskil congregation, we found ourselves compelled by our consciences to provide them with a consistory; but not before having taken about it the advice of the Rev. Ministers at New York and Long Island. These gentlemen unanimously thought that the congregation ought to be provided with a consistory. Before carrying out this advice I tried once more to bring the Consistory of Viskill to better thoughts, and to submit to your Reverences, by reading to them for that purpose your letter of the 3rd of October, 1763, with the resolution of the Synod in it; but again it was in vain, for, after many scoffing abuses and reproaches about Classis and Synod, finally I received from the oldest elder, Jan Brinckerhoff, in the name of the whole consistory, to which the Po'keepsie body had been added, the following answer: They thought that N B (oh! abomination!) commits a sin against the Holy Ghost if he deserts the Coetus (which they considered fully authorized and empowered to all they did and undertook, viz, to examine and to promote independent of Classis and Synod) and if he again submits to your Reverences. Seeing they were incorrigible, I then proceeded with the subordinate members of the congregation to elect a Consistory, and installed them. All the proceedings in regard to it I laid upon the table of our subordinate meeting last June, and it was not only unanimously approved, but I was also heartily thanked for it. Pokeepsie was in similar circumstances, as an elder and a deacon who have not surrendered to the Coetus clearly proved before our meeting. They requested to be provided with a legal and loyal Consistory in the same way as Viskil, and the meeting deputed me and Dr. Koch, Minister at the Camp, to carry it out. How well or badly we have executed our commission your Reverences may see from the enclosed copy of our minutes, which we send for your consideration.

Meanwhile Dr. Blaeuw with thanks declined the call to Viskil and the other congregations; and this compelled the Consistories to proceed to another call, and to give the honor of it to your Reverences, according to their written obligations, a copy of which is enclosed. They do it herewith, hoping, wishing, and praying, that, agreeably to your sanctified discretion, and good will to promote the welfare of the Dutch Zion, as means in the hands of the great Shepherd Jesus, you will send over a pastor for these congregations, who, being a man after God's heart, may direct and pasture them with knowledge and discretion; who, being, like Apollos, mighty in the scripture, can stop the mouths of adversaries; who is of lovable and friendly conversation and intercourse with people, because lack of these qualities has been the first leading cause of the rupture between Dr. Meinema and his congregation; but who above all this, adorns our holy confession of faith with an exemplary, pious, life and walk.

The congregations should now be able to call two pastors, if there were not many who defer signing for a lawful teacher until your Reverences shall have declared this Schoonmaker, so wonderfully promoted, to be unauthorized by our church; which I humbly request to be done soon, so that he may be prevented from preaching and administering the sacraments, and entire quiet and peace may be restored to these congregations by the coming of an authorized pastor. There are also others who delay signing until a preacher comes over on this call, fearing that perhaps another Meinema might come, to whom then they would be bound. Therefore I sincerely pray that Jehovah, directing everything in wisdom, may endow your Reverences with doubled faith and discretion in selecting a teacher for these congregations, and that he will crown with all desired blessings here, and with the reward of faithful servants hereafter, the labor and the unwearied care, which, from time to time, your Reverences have used, and are still employing, for the well being and the advantage of our Dutch churches.

With most devout respect, I sign,
Reverend Fathers and Brothers in Christ
Your obedient servant and brother,
J. C. Fryenmoet V.D.M. in Manor of
Po'keepsie, Livingston, Claverack, and Kinderhook.
the 3rd of Octbr, 1764. (Æt. 43)*

---

* Mr. Fryenmoet had a curious custom of always appending his age to his signature.

In compliance with the request thus forwarded the Classis of Amsterdam selected Rev. Isaac Rysdyck, and the call was accepted by him. He was a native of Holland and was born about 1720. He was educated at the University of Groningen, and, after his admission to the ministry, labored ten or fifteen years in Holland, but in what parish or in what capacity is unknown. There is no copy of the call extended to him in the records now existing, and its precise date cannot be ascertained. But in the record of baptisms by Mr. Rysdyck is an entry of which the following is a translation.

"In 1765, September 22nd, I, Isaac Rysdyck, alone lawful preacher of the Low Dutch Reformed congregation of Poughkeepsie and annexed churches, after presentation of lawful certificates from the Very Rev. Classis of Amsterdam, by whom my call to this congregation was approved, as appears from the instrument of calling registered in the Church book, and from my former congregation and Classis, was installed by Rev. John Casp. Freyenmoet in the congregation of Poughkeepsie." *

Mr. Rysdyck ministered to the two churches from 1765 to 1772, and as Mr. Schoonmaker was ministering to both churches at the same time, each of the two churches, during those years, had two rival pastors and two rival consistories. †

Under these circumstances it must be regarded as fortunate that each of the rival ministers preached on

---

* 1765. Den 22 September ben ik, Isaac Rysdyck, alleen wettig Predikant der Nederduitsche herformde Gemeente van Pougkeepsie cum annexis ecclesiis na vertoning van wettige attestaticn, so van de Hoog Eerw. Classis van Amsterdam, door welke myn Beroeping tot dese Gemeinte geapprobert is, als blykt uyt het Instrument van Beroeping in het Kerkenbock geregisteert, als van myne vorige Gemeinte en Classis, door Dr. Joh. Casp. Freyenmoet, in de Gemeinte van Pougkeepsie ingewydt.

† For these years there are two records of baptisms in different books, one being in the handwriting of Dominie Schoonmaker, and the other in that of Dominie Rysdyck.

alternate Sabbaths in Poughkeepsie and Fishkill. While Dominie Schoonmaker was preaching in one place, Dominie Rysdyck was preaching in the other. In each place the party there favoring the preacher, would attend the service, and the party opposed would stay at home, and thus were avoided collisions which otherwise would have occurred.

In October, 1772, Dr. Isaac Rysdyck presented to the General Synod, "a call made upon him in the congregation of Fishkill, being an adddition to his former call in that place, to serve the congregation of Fishkill in the use alternately of the English and Dutch Languages." The Synod approved the new adjustment, in expectation that his dismission from Poughkeepsie would thereupon be regularly effected, and appointed a committee to effect such dismission.\* The committee, in due time, performed the duty thus assigned, and the record of baptisms by Dr. Rysdyck in Poughkeepsie ends on November, 1773. He continued his labors in the church of Fishkill and the neighboring churches of Hopewell and New Hackensack until very near his decease, which occurred Nov. 20, 1790. He died at New Hackensack, where he resided during the last years of his life, and was buried under the pulpit of the church. The site of the present edifice of the church of New Hackensack is a little north of that occupied by the former edifice, and the place which was under the pulpit of the former edifice is now in the burial ground adjoining the present edifice, and is known as the pastors' plot. There the remains still lie as they were originally deposited, and in the plot there is a monument with this inscription :—†

---

\* Minutes Gen. Synod, Vol. 1, pp. 31, 36, 37.

† For a copy of the inscription the writer is indebted to Rev. W. A. Dumont, pastor of the Church of New Hackensack.

## REV. ISAAC RYSDYCK,
first pastor
of this church,
DIED IN 1790.

He was settled over the churches of Poughkeepsie, Hopewell, Fishkill and New Hackensack in 1765,—and continued his ministry in the three latter churches until his death, when he was buried in front of the pulpit of the former house of worship which stood here from 1766 to 1835.

Mr. Rysdyck was, in his day, considered the most learned theologian in the Dutch church. In addition to his pastoral labors he had charge of a classical school in Fishkill, which was the first of its kind established in Dutchess county. Although he and Rev. Mr. Schoonmaker were of opposite ecclesiastical parties, they maintained friendly relations with each other, and endeavored to allay the prevailing strife. At the meeting of ministers and elders, held in New York in 1771, to devise means for the peace and unity of the churches, both were present and approved the plan of Union which was then adopted.*

6. STEPHEN VAN VOORHEES, 1773–6.

The next pastor was Stephen Van Voorhees, (also written Van Voorhis), for whose history the records of the church furnish but little material. There is not found in them any copy or mention of either his call or his dismission. But in the Minutes of the Synod for October, 1772, it is recorded that he then presented him-

---

* Corwin's Manual and Sprague's Annals.

self to that body for examination and licensure, and that, in his examination, he afforded much satisfaction, and was received among the number of licentiates. In the minutes of the next session, held October, 1773, it is stated that among the calls presented, was "one from the congregation of Poughkeepsie upon Rev. Stephen Van Voorhis," and it was "approved by this Rev. Body." The precise date of his installation is unknown, but in the minutes of the consistory, his name appears as that of the minister, in the meeting held March 22, 1774, and thence continues to appear until May 2, 1776.

After leaving Poughkeepsie he, for a short time, supplied a Reformed Dutch congregation which then existed in Dover, in the eastern part of Dutchess county. From 1776 to 1784 he was the pastor of the church of Rhinebeck; from 1785 to 1788 of the churches of Phillipsburgh, (now Tarrytown,) and Cortlandtown, and from 1788 to 1796 pastor of the Presbyterian churches of Assynpinck and Kingston, in New Jersey. He died November 23, 1796.\*

7. SOLOMON FROELIGH, 1776–80.

Solomon Froeligh (also written Freligh and Freylig), was born May 29, (O. S.) 1730, about two miles east of Red Hook, then in the county of Albany, now in the county of Dutchess. He was licensed by the Synod in October, 1774, and on the 11th of June, 1775, was ordained and installed pastor of the four Reformed Dutch congregations in Queens county, Long Island.

After living there for fifteen months he fled to Hackensack, N. J., and barely escaped being taken prisoner by the British army. In his flight he lost all his worldly

---

\* Corwins' Manual.

goods, including even his books and clothing. As Hackensack was within the region that fell under the control of the British troops, Mr. Froeligh, in company with Dr. Livingston, sought refuge above the Highlands of the Hudson, and accepted an invitation from the then vacant congregations of Poughkeepsie and Fishkill to make a temporary settlement among them. He was not regularly installed over them, and therefore, strictly speaking, was only their "stated supply;" but inasmuch as he remained with them and rendered all the service of a pastor for the space of four years, he was their pastor in fact if not in form.

Among the entries in the records of the church in his own handwriting is one which states that his wife, Rachael Vanderbeck, was, on the 19th of October, 1778, received into the communion of the church on Confession of Faith.

In 1780 he accepted a call from the churches of Millstone and Neshanick in Somerset county, N. J., and was their pastor until 1786, when he accepted a call from the churches of Hackensack and Schraalenbergh in Bergen County, N. J., with whom he remained until the end of his life.

He was appointed Lector in Theology by the General Synod in October, 1792, and Professor of Theology in June, 1797.

In 1822 he headed the secession movement which resulted in the organization of the body known as the True Reformed Dutch Church, and thereupon (June 1823) was, by the Synod, removed from his office as Professor. He died October 8, 1827, in the seventy-eighth year of his age and the fifty-third of his ministry.*

---

* Sprague's Annals.

8. John H. Livingston, 1781-3.

John H. Livingston was born May 30, 1746, in the "Livingston Mansion," * which was built by his father, Henry Livingston, and still stands on the bank of the Hudson a short distance south of Poughkeepsie. He graduated with honor at Yale College, and at twenty went to Holland, and for four years pursued his theological studies at the University of Utrecht. He was licensed by the Classis of Amsterdam in 1769, and, in the following year, returned to this country, and became one of the pastors of the Collegiate Church of New York city.

From that time forth his history is the history of the denomination with which he was connected. Such were his ability and influence, that, among all its ministers, he was conceded to be the foremost, and to him, under God, more than to any other man, was the denomination indebted for the cessation of the intestine strife, which for many years imperiled its existence.

Soon after the outbreak of the Revolutionary War, New York city was occupied by the British forces, and by them two of the three edifices used by the Collegiate Church for worship were sadly abused and desecrated. One, (the North Church,) was used as a hospital and for storage, and the other, (the Middle Church,) was converted first into a prison, and then into a riding school for officers and soldiers. Dr. Livingston, being thus prevented from prosecuting his ministry in New York, removed first to Kingston, thence to Albany, and thence to Livingston Manor, in Columbia county.

In the records of the church of Poughkeepsie occur the following :—

---

* So say his descendants who, until recently, occupied the "Mansion."

"1781, July 9, Resolved to open a subscription list for raising a sum sufficient for the purpose of inviting the Rev. Dr. John H. Livingston, late of the City of New York, but at present at the Manor of Livingston, to become our minister."

"1781, August 4, an invitation was made, and drawn up in proper form in writing, by which the Rev. Dr. Livingston was requested to perform the duties of a minister in the congregation as long as he shall find his situation to be convenient to himself and his family, promising to pay him for his service at the rate of three hundred and fifty bushels of wheat, and fifty pounds in specie per annum."

"1781, August 6, the Rev. Dr. Livingston accepted of this invitation, and is accordingly become the minister of the congregation."

While engaged in his ministry here, Dr. Livingston resided with his father in the Livingston Mansion referred to above. The records of this church show that he was earnest and active, not only in pastoral work, but also in that of extricating the church from serious financial embarrassments in which it had become involved. At the close of his ministry here he wrote in the book of church records the following :—

"It having pleased the LORD to restore peace to America, in consequence of which the exiled inhabitants of the City of New York were permitted to return to their homes,—the Rev. Dr. Livingston took leave of the congregation of Poughkeepsie in an affectionate farewell sermon, Nov. 23, 1783, and opened his ministry again in the City of New York, Dec. 7, 1783.

Thus the church of Poughkeepsie is again become vacant."

Dr. Livingston was subsequently appointed Professor of Didactic and Polemic Theology in the Seminary in New Brunswick, (1784,) and President of Queen's, (now Rutgers,) College, (1810,) and retained these offices until his decease, January 20, 1825. His remains were buried in New Brunswick, and a monument, erected by order of the General Synod, stands over his grave.*

---

* Memoirs of Dr. Livingston, by Alexander Gunn.

## 9. ANDREW GRAY, 1790-4.

The vacancy caused by the departure of Dr. Livingston continued through the seven ensuing years. Many in the congregation were greatly dissatisfied with the consistory for allowing the church to remain so long without a pastor. Among them was Mr. Gilbert Livingston, who, on the 2nd of March, 1790, on account of the negligence of the consistory in this and other matters, laid before that body a formal and written " grievance," which is still preserved among the archives of the church. Soon afterwards a subscription paper, dated June 28, 1790, and with the following heading, was circulated and obtained many signatures :

" We, the Subscribers, residents within the limits of the Reformed Dutch Church of Poughkeepsie, and in the vicinity thereof, being desirous of having Mr. Andrew Gray, (now a Student in Divinity with the Rev$^d$ Doct$^r$ Meyers in New Jersey, when quallifyed for the Ministry,) for the Minister of the Said Church, to dispence the Sacraments, preach the Gospel, catechize the youth, and perform all other sacred ministerial functions as practised heretofore in the Church aforesaid, and to use the English and Dutch languages in his publick exercises in such manner as to the Said Church, from time to time, may be deemed proper and convenient,

THEREFORE, If the Church aforesaid make a call upon the Said Andrew Gray upon the principles above mentioned, and he accepts thereof and becomes the Minister of the aforesaid Church, Do hereby promise to pay and deliver, or cause to be paid and delivered, to the aforesaid Church yearly, and every year, the sums of money and articles written and specified opposite to our Respective names, so long as the Said Andrew Gray continues the Minister of the Church aforesaid, and we remain within the limits of the same, or in the vicinity thereof. Dated June 28th, 1790.

Thus urged and encouraged, the consistory, in the course of the same year, presented a call to the candidate, Andrew Gray. The call itself is not among the records of the church; but there is an entry dated

October 25, 1790, which states that the call had been presented, and that it was "determined to increase the same, and instead of thirty loads, to promise fifty loads" of firewood.

Also, in the Minutes of General Synod, it is recorded that at the meeting of October, 1790, Mr. Andrew Gray was examined and licensed, and that a call was presented to him by the congregation of Poughkeepsie, which was approved; and that arrangements were made for his ordination and installation on the 21st of November, 1790.*

Mr. Gray retained this charge a little more than three years. At the meeting of General Synod, October, 1792, he was appointed a missionary, with instructions to spend six weeks in visiting Hanover and other districts in the valley of the Susquehanna, where were many families of Dutch descent who had moved thither from the valley of the Hudson.† The result showed that, in the appointment of this their first missionary, the Synod had made a wise selection; for his labors were crowned with abundant success, and he himself became so imbued with missionary zeal that he felt it to be alike his duty and his privilege to devote the remainder of his life to missionary work. Accordingly, on November 21, 1793, he sought a release from his charge in Poughkeepsie, and the consistory granted it on account of the very cogent reasons assigned, at the same time expressing themselves as "deeply sensible of the griefs, disappointments and loss the congregation will sustain by this sad occurrence."

In the records of the church the name of Mr. Gray appears, for the last time, as that of the president of the

---

\* Minutes Gen. Synod, Vol. I., pp. 207, 209.

† Minutes Gen. Synod, Vol. I., p. 240.

## Succession of Ministers.

consistory, in the minutes of the meeting held January 2, 1794. He spent the remaining years of his life in preaching the Gospel, and establishing churches, on the outskirts of civilization in Pennsylvania and central New York, and died in 1819.*

10. CORNELIUS BROWER, 1794–1808.

Cornelius Brower (also written Bronwer), was born in New York city in 1770, graduated from Columbia College in 1792, studied under Dr. Livingston, and was licensed by the Classis of New York in 1793. The call to him from the church of Poughkeepsie is dated February 3, 1794, and is attested by Rev. Nicholas Van Vranken, then pastor of the church of Fishkill.

He was ordained and installed July 13, 1794, and was the pastor of the church until the regular meeting of the Classis, April 19, 1808, when the pastoral connection was dissolved.

Mr. Brower supplied the church of Hyde Park from 1812 to 1815, was professor in the High School in Utica from 1815 to 1833, and served as supply in several neighboring churches until his death in 1845.†

11. CORNELIUS C. CUYLER, 1809–33.

Cornelius C. Cuyler was born in Albany, February 15, 1783. The middle letter was inserted in his name in order to distinguish him from six contemporaries of the same surname, all of whom were called Cornelius. He graduated at Union College in 1806, studied under Drs. Bassett and Livingston, and was licensed by the Classis of Schenectady in 1808. The call to him from the church of Poughkeepsie was dated October 18, 1808, and attested by Cornelius D. Westbrook, then pastor of

---

* Corwin's Manual, and Dr. Mabon in "Centennial Discourses."
† Corwin's Manual.

the church of Fishkill. The ordination and installation took place January 2, 1809.

The ministry of Dr. Cuyler was so eminently fruitful that it may be called the turning point in the history of the church. The records show that, when he came, all the affairs of the church were in a confused and unsatisfactory condition, and that there were but forty-three members in full communion. Under his vigorous administration order was soon brought out of confusion, and the membership rapidly increased. It was during his pastorate that the third edifice was erected, in 1822, in order to meet the wants of the enlarged congregation. At the close of his ministry here the reported number of members was 402, and the church was united, active and vigorous.

While in charge of this church he received several calls to other churches, among which was one from the Collegiate church of New York (1814); but such was his affection for this church, and so great was the blessing vouchsafed to his labors in it, that he declined them all. In 1833, however, although he was then only fifty years of age, he felt that his bodily strength was no longer adequate to the service needed by such an extensive congregation, and, greatly to the sorrow of his loving and beloved people, accepted a call from the second Presbyterian church of Philadelphia. He was dismissed from Poughkeepsie, December 17, 1833, and continued to serve the church in Philadelphia until his decease, August 31, 1850.*

12. SAMUEL A. VAN VRANKEN, 1834–7.

Samuel A. Van Vranken was the son of Rev. Nicholas Van Vranken, for many years the pastor of the church of Fishkill, and was born in Fishkill, February 20, 1792.

---

* Commemorative Discourse, by Rev. Joseph H. Jones.

He graduated at Union College in 1815, and from the Theological Seminary in New Brunswick in 1817, and in the latter year was licensed by the Classis of New Brunswick. He served the united churches of Middletown and Freehold in Monmouth County, N. J., from 1818 to 1826, and the church of Freehold alone from 1826 to 1834.

He was called to the church of Poughkeepsie May 12, 1834, and was installed on the second Tuesday of the following September. He was dismissed November 21, 1837, in order to take charge of the Broome Street Church in New York city, where he remained until 1841, when he was appointed Professor of Didactic and Polemic Theology in the Seminary in New Brunswick, in which office he continued until his decease, January 1, 1861.*

13. ALEXANDER M. MANN, 1838–57.

Rev. Alexander M. Mann was born in the city of Philadelphia, March 16, 1808. He was the sixth of twelve children, two of whom, beside himself, are still living. He removed with his parents to Somerville, N. J., in 1813, and there spent the largest part of his boyhood. He united with the church when a little more than fourteen years of age, and soon after began to study for the ministry.

After a preparatory course in the academy at Somerville, he entered the Junior Class of Rutgers College in 1825, graduated from the college in 1827, from the Theological Seminary in New Brunswick in April, 1730, and in September of the same year was licensed by the Classis of New Brunswick. Immediately afterwards he was commissioned by the Domestic Missionary Society of the Reformed church to take charge of a church in Ithaca, N. Y., just organized, with 20 families and 32 communicants. Here his labors were greatly blessed,

---

* McClintock and Strong, Cyclopædia.

and, in seven years, the church had grown to 100 families, with an average yearly addition of 24 to membership. In 1837, for personal reasons, and against the desires of his people, he resigned this charge. A call was soon received from the church of West Troy, and an acceptance was given, conditioned on a trial of the field. Not being sufficiently encouraged by his labors there, he accepted the call extended to him by the church of Poughkeepsie, February 5, 1838, assumed charge of the church immediately, and was formally installed as pastor on the 22nd day of May following.

It was during his pastorate of nearly twenty years that the third parsonage was built, the Second church was formed, by members dismissed for that purpose, and the third church edifice was first renovated, and afterwards destroyed by fire.

Dr. Mann was dismissed from the church of Poughkeepsie, June 15, 1857. After leaving Poughkeepsie, he was for four years pastor of the church of Hoboken, N. J., and then accepted a call from the Presbyterian Church of Freemansburg, N. Y., where he also remained about four years. Then, feeling the burden of advancing years, he resigned, and has since been without pastoral charge. He has resided for several years in Farmer Village, Seneca Co., N. Y., and, until disabled by bodily infirmities, rendered excellent service in supplying vacant churches in the neighborhood.

He is now totally blind, and is the only survivor of those who were in the ministry of the Reformed church when he entered it, nearly 63 years ago. Dr. Mann was President of the General Synod at the Session of 1851, and received the degree of D.D. from the University of Rochester in 1856.*

---

* From a biographical sketch prepared for this work by Rev. F. W. Palmer, under the supervision of Dr. Mann.

## 14. GEORGE M. McECKRON, 1858-67.

George Mairs McEckron (originally McEachron), was born September 3, 1826, in Argyle, N. Y., was graduated at Union College in 1848, studied theology at the Associate Reformed Seminary in Newburgh, and was licensed June 30, 1851, by the Washington Presbytery of the Associate Reformed Church. He was ordained and installed pastor of the Associate Reformed Church of Mongaup Valley, Sullivan County, N. Y., January 12, 1853, and retained this charge until April 20, 1858, when he tendered his resignation and the pastoral relation was dissolved. The call to him from the First Reformed church of Poughkeepsie, was dated March 26, 1858. He was installed September 7, 1858, and his pastorate extended over nearly nine years. During those years there were two notable revivals, one in 1858, and the other in 1866. In the latter year eighty-five persons were received into the church on confession of faith.

Mr. McEckron sent his resignation to the consistory February 18, 1867, and the pastoral relation was dissolved by the Classis February 21. From October 13, 1868, to December 16, 1868, he was pastor of the Presbyterian Church of New Hamburgh, and from February 7, 1869, to October 10, 1871, was pastor of the Westminster Presbyterian Church in New York city. He was without a charge until 1874 or 1875, when he became acting pastor of the Congregational church of Parkville, Long Island. His name, as that of acting pastor, first appears on the records of that church January 13, 1875, and his resignation was tendered and accepted July 27, 1877. While thus serving a Congregational church, he still retained his connection with the Presbytery of New York; but on the 3rd of October, 1881, the Presbytery received a communication from him, stating that he had withdrawn from the Presbyterian Ministry, and requesting that his name be stricken from the roll of Presbytery.* The request was granted and his name was erased. He died, in New York city, July 14, 1884.†

15. A. P. VAN GIESON, 1867-.

The call to the present pastor, Rev. A. P. Van Gieson, was dated August 6, 1867. He began his labors in the church on the first Sunday of October following, and was formally installed as pastor at the stated meeting of Classis, held in the church on the fifteenth of the same month, (October 15, 1867).

SUCCESSION OF ELDERS AND DEACONS. 1716-1892.

The first elders and deacons were doubtless elected by the votes of the male communicants. Such is the requirement of the Constitution of the Reformed church now, in the forming of new churches, and such has been the custom from time immemorial.

From this first election until 1747, it is uncertain whether the officers were elected by the members of the church, or by the consistory. The records simply state that from time to time the elders and deacons were installed, and say nothing definite concerning the manner of their election. At a meeting held December 9, 1741, the following action was taken:

" The old and new consistories have thought proper to give order, that every year on the first Tuesday in the month of May, for maintaining order in the Christian congregation, an election be held for choosing elders and deacons and church masters, according to the rules of the Synod of Dort, according to the wisdom which the Lord our God may continue to give to them."‡

---

* Dr. Scouller's Manual and Records of Churches and Presbyteries.

† The Courier, Poughkeepsie, July 20, 1884.

‡ Desem. den 9 dagh hebben de oude en nuwe Kerkenrat Goet Gedocht om een order te maken om alle yaren een verkising te maken op de eersste

## Succession of Elders and Deacons. 1716–1892.

This is ambiguous, but rather seems to intimate that the election was to be by the "Christian congregation."

In 1747, the record is different, and is as follows:

"Consistory meeting held, and, after prayer, Gysbert Pele and Louwereus Van Kleeck were elected elders, and Pytter Van Kleeck and Pytter La Roy as deacons, and were installed February 8th."*

The record for the years following is of a similar character, and from this it is evident that in and after the year 1747, the election was not by the members of the church, but by the consistory. The elders and deacons already in office chose their own successors. This was one of the grounds of complaint specified by Mr. Gilbert Livingston in his "Grievance" presented to the then ruling consistory in 1790, and referred to on page 69. He urged that the members of the consistory, by electing their own successors, were acting contrary to the requirements of the Confession of Faith, and usurping a right and privilege which belonged to the church.

No change, however, was made until September 23, 1822, when at a meeting of consistory presided over by the Rev. Dr. Cuyler, the following resolution was adopted, viz:—

"*Resolved*, That this Consistory are of opinion that the present mode of electing Elders and Deacons ought not to be continued in this church, and, therefore, ask leave of Classis to have the mode of election altered, so that the elections be held by the male members of the church in good standing."

The leave thus asked was granted by the Classis at its regular meeting, held on the day following, and thence-

---

dingsdagh in de mant van mey om de christelike Ghementen in order te houden om ouderlingen in diyakeneu in Kerkmesters te Kisen volligens it Regt van de Sinode van dort, volligens de Kennis die onse Heeren God har blift in te geven.

* 11 Jan. 1747 Kerken-Raadt gehouden en syn na aanroeping van's H. H. Naam verkoren tot ouderlingen Gysbert Pele en Louwerens van Kleeck, en tot Diakenen Pytter van Kleek en Pytter La Roy, en bevestigt 8 Febr.

forth the elders and deacons were elected by the male members of the church until 1871. In that year, by order of consistory, the female members of the church were invited to take part in the elections, and thenceforth, until 1891, the officers of the church were chosen by all the members, without distinction of sex or age. At the meeting of General Synod held in June, 1891, the Constitution of the Reformed Church was so amended as to restrict the privilege of choosing elders and deacons to "the members of the church in full communion who shall have attained the age of eighteen years"; and this is the rule which is now in force.

A very large majority of the elders and deacons of the church have been re-elected several times, and, either continuously or with interruptions, have served in their respective offices several terms of two years each. In the succession given below the re-elections are omitted, and the number opposite to each name indicates the date of the first election as deacon or elder.

### ELDERS.

| | | | |
|---|---|---|---|
| Machiel Parmentier, | 1716 | Johannes Ten Broek, | 1750 |
| Pieter Dubois, | 1716 | Christoffell Van Bommell, | 1753 |
| Jan Osterum, | 1718 | Henry Livingston, | 1753 |
| Johannes Ter Bosch, | 1720 | Petrus Laroy, | 1753 |
| Barent Van Kleeck, | 1721 | Hendric Oostrum | 1754 |
| Jan Buys, | 1721 | Barent Lewis, | 1754 |
| Pieter Parmentier, | 1724 | Johannes Swartwout, | 1755 |
| Johannes Van Kleeck, | 1731 | Henricus Hageman, | 1764 |
| Elias Van Beenschooten, | 1733 | Pieter Van Kleeck, | 1764 |
| Frans Laroy, | 1739 | Hiskia Hooghteelingh, | 1765 |
| Mateus du bois, | 1741 | Johannes Fort, | 1766 |
| Jacobus Van den Bogert, | 1741 | Isaac Hageman, | 1766 |
| Gysbert Pels, | 1747 | Gulyn Ackerman, | 1767 |
| Louwerens Van Kleeck, | 1747 | Jacobus Degraef, | 1767 |
| Jacobus Stoutenburg, | 1748 | Johannes Freer, | 1768 |
| Ezekiel Masten, | 1748 | Elias Van Beenschooten, | 1770 |
| Johannes Kankeli. | 1749 | Simeon Freer, | 1771 |
| Aart Middog, | 1749 | Denie Oostrom, | 1772 |

## Elders.

| | |
|---|---|
| Tobias Stoutenburgh, | 1774 |
| Richard Snedeker, | 1774 |
| Gilbert Livingston, | 1774 |
| Jacobus Freer, | 1777 |
| Moses Degraef, | 1778 |
| Leonard Van Kleeck, | 1778 |
| Johannes Van Kleeck, | 1779 |
| John Conklin, | 1779 |
| Pieter Lewis, | 1780 |
| Gulian Ackerman, | 1781 |
| William Stoutenburgh, | 1781 |
| Peter Tappen, | 1781 |
| Egbert Benson, | 1782 |
| Peter Schryver, | 1783 |
| John Freer, | 1783 |
| Isaac Romine, | 1783 |
| Henry Hagaman, | 1787 |
| John Van Kleeck, | 1791 |
| Myndert Van Kleeck, | 1792 |
| Peter Low, | 1792 |
| Abraham Sleight, | 1793 |
| John Baily, | 1793 |
| Peter Connell, | 1793 |
| Joost Westervelt, | 1794 |
| Albertus Scryver, | 1795 |
| Wines Manny, | 1796 |
| Peter Cornell, | 1796 |
| Peter DeRiemer, | 1797 |
| Jacob R. Duryee, | 1799 |
| Benjamin Westervelt, | 1801 |
| Joseph Westervelt, | 1804 |
| Isaac Romaine, | 1804 |
| Abraham Pells, | 1805 |
| Paul Schenck, | 1806 |
| Peter LeRoy, | 1809 |
| Cornelius Swartwout, | 1809 |
| John Pells, | 1809 |
| David Carpenter, | 1810 |
| Adrian Covenhoven, | 1810 |
| Samuel Matthews, | 1810 |
| Henry Barnes, | 1811 |
| Abraham G. Storm, | 1811 |
| Hendrick Wiltsey, | 1812 |
| Robert Forrest, | 1814 |
| Evert A. Pells, | 1815 |
| Simeon DeGraff, | 1816 |
| John M. Cook, | 1817 |
| John V. B. Varick, | 1820 |
| William Bell, | 1821 |
| Joseph Harris, | 1823 |
| Peter A. Schryver, | 1824 |
| Michael T. Heyser, | 1824 |
| Joshua Bishop, | 1824 |
| Lawrence I. Van Kleeck, | 1826 |
| Thomas W. Tallmadge, | 1827 |
| Isaac Roosevelt, | 1831 |
| Abraham Overbagh, | 1835 |
| Charles P. Adriance, | 1836 |
| John C. Van Valkenburgh, | 1837 |
| Cornelius Westervelt, | 1839 |
| Aaron Low, | 1841 |
| Phillip Ostrander, | 1842 |
| Abraham Snydam, | 1843 |
| Dr. John Barnes, | 1843 |
| John Bodden, | 1843 |
| Josiah Burritt, | 1844 |
| William Broas, | 1850 |
| Henry D. Varick, | 1852 |
| Elisha Conover, | 1852 |
| David C. Foster, | 1853 |
| Herman J. Jewett, | 1856 |
| William Brownell, | 1856 |
| Charles M. Pelton, | 1857 |
| Daniel R. Thompson, | 1858 |
| Eliphalet Buel, | 1859 |
| Dr. Elvy Deyo, | 1859 |
| James Alexander, | 1863 |
| John H. Matthews, | 1865 |
| Warren Skinner, | 1869 |
| Henry L. Young, | 1871 |
| Milton A. Fowler, | 1872 |
| Lewis D. Barnes, | 1877 |
| Charles C. More, | 1879 |
| Marvin O. Dutton, | 1886 |
| John W. Pelton, | 1891 |

## DEACONS.

| | |
|---|---|
| Elias Van Bunschooten, . 1716 | Hendrik Pels, . . . . 1769 |
| Pieter Parmentier, . . . 1716 | Isaac Kool, . . . . . . 1769 |
| Johannes Van Kleeck, . . 1718 | Jan Oostrom, . . . . 1770 |
| Jacobus Van den Bogoord, 1720 | Isaak Romeyn, . . . . 1770 |
| Frans Le Roy, . . . . . 1721 | Myndert Van Denbogart, 1774 |
| Louwerens Van Kleeck, 1721 | Henry S. Pells, . . . 1774 |
| Myndert Van den Bogaart, 1724 | Isaac Romeyn, Jr., . . 1774 |
| Pieter Van Kleeck, . . 1731 | Johan Barrack, . . . 1774 |
| Henry Van der Burgh, 1732 | Henry Livingston, . . 1777 |
| Henricus Pells, . . . 1733 | Jacob Low, . . . . 1777 |
| Johannes Tappen, . . 1739 | Garret Van Vliet, . . 1778 |
| Abraham De Graef, . . 1739 | Petrus Van Vliet, . . 1778 |
| Francis Filkin, . . . . 1741 | Bernardus Swartwout, 1778 |
| Gilbert Pealing, . . . 1742 | Garret Van Bomel, . . 1779 |
| Pieter Vielen, . . . . 1742 | Lucas Stoutenburgh, . 1779 |
| Pytter Van Kleeck, . . 1747 | Nicolaus Anthony, . . 1780 |
| Pytter Laroy, . . . . 1747 | Robert Hoffman, . . 1780 |
| Herri Libbeston, . . . 1748 | Myndert Van Kleeck, . 1781 |
| Augustenus Turk, . . 1748 | Johannes Schryver, . 1781 |
| Simeon Freer, . . . . 1749 | Isaac Conklin, . . . 1782 |
| Matthew Van Keuren, 1749 | Aaron Low, . . . . 1782 |
| Johannes Lewis, . . . 1750 | Cornelius Westervelt, . 1783 |
| Teunis Voos, . . . . . 1750 | Wines Manny, . . . 1783 |
| Hendrikus Hageman, . 1752 | Abraham Fort, . . . 1783 |
| Elias Du Bois, . . . . 1752 | Benjamin Westervelt, . 1787 |
| Roelof Oostrum, . . . 1752 | Henry Livingston, Jr., . 1787 |
| Abraham Swartwout, . 1752 | Joost Westervelt, . . 1791 |
| Damon Palmentier, . . 1754 | Peter Connell, . . . 1791 |
| Johannes Rynders, . . 1754 | Peter Leroy, . . . . 1791 |
| William Cyffer, . . . 1755 | Gabriel Ellison, . . . 1792 |
| Moses Verfeele, . . . 1755 | Jacob Duryee, . . . 1792 |
| Isaac Hegeman, . . . 1763 | Albert Scryver, . . . 1793 |
| John Kancklin, . . . 1763 | Cornelius Swartwout, . 1793 |
| Guleyn Ackerman, . . 1764 | Peter I. Vanderburg, . 1793 |
| Jacobus De Graef, . . 1764 | Abraham Pells, . . . 1795 |
| Johannes Freer, . . . 1765 | Jacob K. Duryee, . . 1795 |
| Denie Oostrom, . . . 1765 | John Low, . . . . 1795 |
| David Ackerman, . . 1766 | John Stoutenburg, . . 1796 |
| Jacobus Freer, . . . 1766 | Bernardus Van Kleeck, 1797 |
| James Agmoedie, . . 1767 | Hendrick Masten, . . 1798 |
| Isaac Van Bunschooten, 1767 | Adrian Covenhoven, . 1798 |
| Moses Degraef, . . . 1768 | John L. Van Kleeck, . 1799 |

## Deacons.    81

| | |
|---|---|
| Paul Schenck, | 1799 |
| Samuel Matthews, | 1801 |
| John Rogers, | 1801 |
| Michael Tomkins, | 1804 |
| John Pells, | 1805 |
| Abraham Van Wagener, | 1805 |
| Henry Barnes, | 1809 |
| Abraham G. Storms, | 1809 |
| Roelof Van Voorhees, | 1809 |
| Hendrick Wiltsey, | 1810 |
| Evert A. Pells, | 1810 |
| John M. Cook, | 1810 |
| Daniel Hebard, | 1811 |
| Benjamin Howland, | 1811 |
| John H. Dubois, | 1811 |
| Peter A. Scryver, | 1812 |
| Robert Forrest, | 1812 |
| David Ring, | 1813 |
| George T. Brinckerhoff, | 1813 |
| Thomas W. Tallmadge, | 1814 |
| Isaac H. Palmatier, | 1814 |
| Joshua Bishop, | 1814 |
| George Bloom, | 1815 |
| Halstead Price, | 1815 |
| Ezra Boughton, | 1816 |
| William Bell, | 1817 |
| Abraham Ver Valin, | 1818 |
| Peter Pells, | 1818 |
| Frederick Phelps, | 1820 |
| Joseph Parmalee, | 1821 |
| Michael T. Heyser, | 1822 |
| John Dearing, Jr., | 1822 |
| John C. Van Valkenburgh, | 1823 |
| Richard T. Van Wyck, | 1823 |
| George Swan, | 1824 |
| Abraham Van Wagenen, | 1824 |
| Isaac Roosevelt, | 1825 |
| David Ver Valin, | 1825 |
| Abraham Overbagh, | 1826 |
| Sidney M. Livingston, | 1826 |
| Peter H. Lawson, | 1827 |
| Amos T. De Groff, | 1828 |
| Jacob Boerum, | 1831 |
| William Brownell, | 1831 |
| Charles P. Adriance, | 1832 |
| Jacob Rowe, | 1833 |
| William Broas, | 1835 |
| James W. Bogardus, | 1835 |
| Cornelius Westervelt, | 1835 |
| Ezekiel Jewell, | 1835 |
| Elisha L. Haley, | 1836 |
| Phillip Ostrander, | 1836 |
| Aaron Low, | 1838 |
| John Van Wyck, | 1838 |
| Casper D. Smith, | 1839 |
| Abraham A. Davis, | 1839 |
| David C. Foster, | 1840 |
| Cornelius Cornell, | 1840 |
| Daniel D. Jones, | 1841 |
| Elisha Conover, | 1842 |
| James Trivett, | 1842 |
| Herman J. Jewett, | 1842 |
| Isaac H. Coller, | 1843 |
| Albert Brett, | 1843 |
| Henry D. Varick, | 1844 |
| Stephen Uhl, | 1844 |
| Charles M. Pelton, | 1844 |
| William H. Bradley, | 1845 |
| David Boerum, | 1845 |
| John Van Keuren, | 1849 |
| John Hagaman, | 1850 |
| Norman M. Finlay, | 1850 |
| Dr. Elvy Deyo, | 1851 |
| Barnard D. Van Kleeck, | 1852 |
| Daniel R. Thompson, | 1853 |
| David B. Lent, Jr., | 1854 |
| William Simmons, | 1856 |
| John C. McNeil, | 1856 |
| George W. Payne, | 1858 |
| John R. Leslie, | 1858 |
| Jonathan Ransom, | 1859 |
| Charles Carman, | 1859 |
| Cornelius S. Van Wyck, | 1860 |
| William H. Broas, | 1861 |
| George B. Adriance, | 1862 |
| Charles J. Howell, | 1862 |
| John K. Mandeville, | 1863 |

| | | | |
|---|---|---|---|
| Lewis D. Barnes, | 1865 | L. F. Read, | 1879 |
| John W. Miller, | 1868 | J. Collins Pumpelly, | 1880 |
| Milton A. Fowler, | 1868 | Charles D. Johnson, | 1880 |
| John V. H. Miller, | 1872 | Chester A. George, | 1881 |
| John W. Pelton, | 1872 | James M. Hadden, | 1882 |
| Charles W. Bradley, | 1873 | Marvin O. Dutton, | 1885 |
| Samuel W. Buck, | 1875 | George W. Polk, | 1886 |
| Nathan D. Barrows, | 1877 | Henry E. Losey, | 1886 |
| Charles C. More, | 1878 | Charles R. Dickinson, | 1891 |

SUNDAY SCHOOL.

The American Sunday School Union was not organized until 1824, and at that time Sunday Schools were few, and by many excellent Christian people were looked upon with disfavor. They were regarded as an innovation, and even as a desecration of the Lord's Day.

Reports of Sunday Schools in the Reformed Dutch churches do not appear on the minutes of General Synod until 1835, when it was resolved that "the churches in our communion be earnestly solicited to bestow increased diligence on the religious education of the young;" that the consistories "labor to render the Sabbath School institutions as profitable as may be, by correcting defects which may appear;" and "that, for the sake of diffusing information on the interesting subject, and of receiving the happy results of observation and experience, a report be made annually to the several Classes, of the manner in which the schools are conducted, the number of scholars belonging to them, the average attendance of the pupils, and the state of the school as it regards improvement in knowledge and piety, and that the substance of such report be embodied with the statistical reports of the churches on the minutes of the several Classes."

The first report to Synod of the Sunday School of the Church of Poughkeepsie appears in the minutes of the Synod of 1839, (at which time Rev. Dr. Mann was the pastor,) and states that the church had then but one school, and that the number of pupils was 165, and the average attendance 120. This, however, does not indicate the beginning of regular Sunday School work in the church, for in the minutes of the consistory appears an annual report to the Classis for 1825-6, which is signed by Rev. Dr. Cuyler, and states that "Catechetical exercises, prayer meetings, and Sabbath Schools have been maintained." So far as is known, this is the first mention of the Sunday School which occurs in the records of the church and from the phraseology it is evident that at that date there were several schools, (doubtless in different neighborhoods of the then scattered congregation,) and that one or more of them had been "maintained" for some time, (probably for some years,) prior to 1825.

Many of the early records of the Sunday School itself have been lost, and those which remain are imperfect. They simply state the attendance from Sabbath to Sabbath, and do not contain either the minutes of the proceedings of teachers and officers, or any list of officers.

It appears in them, incidentally, that Robert Forrest was superintendent in 1826, that John Thompson * was secretary in 1829 and 1830, that Jacob Rowe was superintendent in 1835, E. L. Haley in 1837, and Robert For-

---

* Many of the friends of the Hon. John Thompson in his later years will easily recognize his style in the latter of the following entries, which are in his own handwriting :—

"Nov. 1, 1829. I entered this morning upon the duties of the office of secretary of the school, to which I have been appointed by its officers."

JOHN THOMPSON.

"Feby 21, 1830. Weather very pleasant, and while the invigorating beams of the natural sun cheer and animate the inhabitants of earth, we can, at times, feel the beams of the sun of righteousness as they dawn upon the heart."

rest again in 1839. Here there is a complete break in the records for several years. Members of the church, now of mature age, who, during those years, attended the Sunday School as teachers or scholars, state, from recollection, that it was then superintended by Jonathan Ransom, Aaron Low, and Henry D. Varick.

After the break, the records are kept more systematically, and show the following succession of superintendents :—

   Daniel R. Thompson, 1853–63.
   John H. Mathews, 1863–75.
   Henry S. Jewett, 1875–6.
   Milton A. Fowler, 1876–   .

At the date of the last annual report the total enrollment of the school was 354.

## CHURCH EDIFICES.

The church has erected and occupied four edifices in succession.

### First Edifice. 1723–1760.

Steps towards the erection of the first edifice were taken soon after the organization of the church in 1716. In the earliest Church Masters' book are copies of subscription lists which were circulated in 1717, bearing (in Dutch) the following heading :—

"WHEREAS, The neighbors and inhabitants of Poughkeepsie desire to build a house of the Lord at Poughkeepsie, the elders and deacons have deemed it advisable to ask every one of the Christian congregation what each shall be willing to give towards the building of the same, and so much here to subscribe."*

---

* Nademael De Beure & in woondere van Pogkeepse genegen zyn Een huys Des Heeren te bouwen op Pogkeepse Soo heeft het De ouderlingen & Diakenen goed gedaght Een Elder van de Cristelike gemeente te versoeke wat Elleck Sal gelieven to geeven tot op bouen vant selve En Soo Veel hier onder to Tekene.

The subscriptions which are appended are partly in money and partly in days' work. The highest subscriptions in money are sixty guilders each. * The sum total in money amounted to 1,427 guilders. The sum total of days' work subscribed was 61, which were estimated at six guilders per day, and, therefore, as equivalent to 366 guilders.

There is also another list of subscriptions amounting to 648 guilders for the construction of the arched pulpit, "Doophuisee,"† and magistrates' seats.

In the same Church Masters' book is the following entry, (in Dutch) August, (day not specified) 1723.

"The places in the church are given out by the chosen Church Masters, Leonard Lewis, Barendt Van Kleeck and Pieter Palmetier, viz :—to every one herewith set down and to their heirs forever, also to their assigns being church members, and at the price as hereby set down, being for the payment of the cost of the building of the church."‡

This is immediately followed by a list giving the names of persons, the number of sittings assigned to

---

* Mr. Jonathan Pierson, in his History of the Church of Schenectady, says, (pp. 62 and 180,) " The money of accounts of the Dutch was the guilder or florin, and stuyver, 20 of the latter to one of the former. There were the guilder sewant, (wampum,) and the guilder beaver ; the latter, of the value of about 40 cents, or three times that of the former. The guilder of accounts was commonly valued at one shilling New York currency."

In the books of the church of Poughkeepsie at about 1740 the guilder disappears, and the accounts are in pounds, shillings and pence, New York currency—the pound being equal to $2.50.

† " Doophuisje," (literally, "Little Baptism House,") was the name used to designate the space between the pulpit and the railing in front of it, in which the minister stood administering the sacrament of baptism.

‡ Aug., 1723. De plaetsen in De Kerck Zyn uyt gegeven door de Verkorene Kerkmeesters Leonard Lewis, Barendt Van Kleeck & pieter palmetier. viz. Aen Een Eider Neven gestelt en aen haer Erfgename Voor Ewigh ook aen haer Assigneurs Zynde Ledemate, en tot De preis als hier by gestelt zynde tot voldoening van de oncoste van De Kerckt Bouen.

each, the number of the bench or pew in which the sittings were located, and the prices of the sittings.

A little later in the same book appears the following receipt, in English ; so curious that it is worthy of transcription :—

1724, April 22. Wie unther weritten William Ennis & John Slater acknowledge to be fully Satesfied and paid for all the Joyners work Dun to the Church that is for the arch Pulput Doway Cannupe and all the Seets made in the Church the sum of Sexty pound 9s by Coll. Leonard Lewis, Capt. Barent Van Kleeck and Mr. Pieter Palmetier as Witness our hands.

WILLIAM ENNIS,<br>JOHN SLATER.

From the foregoing extracts, it is evident that subscriptions for the building of the first house of worship were obtained in 1717, that the house was completed and occupied in 1723, (eight years before the coming of the first pastor,) and that in 1724 the bill for work done to the interior of the house had been presented and paid.

Concerning the location of this first edifice many wild and unfounded assertions have hitherto been made. Mr. Smith, in his History of Dutchess County, asserts that it was on the north side of Main street. Even so careful a historian as Mr. Benson J. Lossing, in a paper read in Poughkeepsie before the Young Men's Christian Association, on the evening of November 13, 1876, and published in the Dutchess Farmer of December 12, 1876, asserted that the edifice " stood on the north side of Main street, a little east of the Poughkeepsie Hotel, where its burying ground may yet be seen."* Mr. Henry Dubois Bailey, in his Historical Sketches, published in Fishkill in 1874, says (p. 297) that it "stood in the centre of what is now known as Market Street."

---

* Mr. Smith and Mr. Lossing doubtless had in mind the second edifice, (concerning which their assertion as to location is true,) and were not aware that there had been another preceding it.

## Church Edifices. 87

All these assertions are erroneous, as appears from the following evidence, by which the location of the church is determined beyond question.

First, is the deed dated December 26, 1716, by which Jacobus Van den Bogert conveyed to Barent Van Kleeck and others a piece or lot of ground " for the proper and only use, benefitt and behoof of the Inhabitance and Naberhood of pochkepsen aforesaid to bild and maentaen a proper Mieteng hous to worship the one and Thrieeonely God according to the Ruels and Methods as it is agried and Concludett by the Sinode National kept at Dordregt in the year 1618 and 1619, and that in the Neder Dutch Lingoo."

The lot thus conveyed is described as " Scituated Lyieng and being in pochkeepseng" and "butted and Boundett on the Nort Sid to the Rood that runs to the Eastard" and " on the west along the Rood that runs to the Sout" and as " a Corner Lott in Lenght one hunderid and fifty foot and in breth one hunderid and fifty foot, beieng a four squaer Lodt."

The " Rood to the Eastard," thus given as one boundary, is now Main street, and the " Rood to the Sout," given as another boundary, is now Market street and the corner lot thus conveyed is on the corner of Main and Market streets opposite to the Court House, and is that on which the City National Bank and some adjoining buildings now stand. The lot was given for the express purpose of building a meeting house thereon. The church had then no other piece of land on which to build, and as the work of building was begun soon after the conveyance of the lot, it must be inferred that the edifice was built on that lot.

Second. That this inference is correct is proven by another deed, dated June 16, 1756, by which Peter Van Kleeck conveyed to Gale Yelverton a lot with thirty yards frontage, on the north side of what is now Main street, and in the deed is called "The East Lane." The lot thus conveyed was afterwards (1760) conveyed to the church and is known to be the thirty yards on the north side of Main street adjoining and east of the Nelson House Annex, formerly the Poughkeepsie Hotel. It is directly opposite to the corner of Market and Main streets. But, in the deed referred to, this lot is described as being "Opposite to the North end of the church." It follows that the north end of the church was opposite to the lot described, and this locates the church on or near the corner of Market and Main streets.

Third, The southern and eastern boundaries of the corner lot on which the church stood have remained unchanged, and are well known at the present time, and, by measurements from them, it appears that the lot, as originally conveyed, extended westward about eleven feet beyond the line of the curbstone of Market street at the corner of Main, and northward about the same distance beyond the line of the curbstone in Main street. In other words, in the widening of the old South Road into the present Market street, and of the old East Lane into the present Main street, a strip about eleven feet wide, plus the sidewalk, has been cut off from each of those two sides of the lot.

It is thus evident, from documents of unquestioned authority, that the first edifice stood on a lot one hundred and fifty feet square on the corner of Main and Market streets, with one end towards Main street, and that, if it was built on or near the western line of the lot, it may have covered a few feet of what is now Market street.

Concerning the materials of which it was constructed the records give no direct information. The accounts, however, show that payments were made for lumber, and nails, and a lime kiln, and make no mention of brick. Hence, it may be inferred, with a good degree of certainty, that the material was not brick; that it may possibly have been wood; but that more probably it was stone.

The following extracts show conclusively that the edifice was supplied with a gallery, that a new gallery was constructed about 1741, that the church was at the same time newly roofed, and that while the seats on the main floor were rented, those in the gallery were free.

"November, A. D. 1741. Then are these expenses incurred by the congregation for roofing the church and making a new gallery therein."*

The items immediately follow, and among them is a charge of six shillings for two "pilaren" (pillars).

November, A. D. 1741, Hereunder stand the persons subscribed what they have promised for to roof the church and a free gallery for the Congregation."† (The list of subscriptions follows.)

A rudely drawn plan of the ground floor of the edifice is found on page 44 of the Church Masters' book, and a reduced copy of it is presented on the following page.

From this it appears that there were 26 pews, exclusive of the benches or pews along the walls, three being on either side of the pulpit, and two lines of ten each in front of the pulpit, and separated by the single aisle. The narrow space, about midway in the plan, probably represents a cross aisle, giving access to the seats along the wall. One of the pews against the wall is, in the

---

\* Novemr Annog domini 1741 dan is dese onkosten van de ghementen ghedan an de Kerk hem te decken ende een neuwe galdery in te maken.

† Novemr Annog domini 1741 hier onder stan de personen onder ghetickent wat sei Beloft hebben voor de Kerk te decken ende een vrije Galdery vor de gemente.

GROUND PLAN OF FIRST EDIFICE.

plan, marked "Justises Gestoelte" *i. e.* "Magistrates' Pew," and there is record of payment for the hinges and lock on its door.*

From this plan an approximate estimate can be made of the dimensions of this first edifice. Allowing three feet for each pew, (which, however, is a very liberal estimate,) it was about 40 to 50 feet long and about 30 feet wide. Mr. Henry Dubois Bailey, in his "Historical Tales and Sketches," thus describes it. "The material of which the church was built was stone, with a hipped roof, and a moderate tower in front. The tower extended above the peak of the roof a short distance, and there the bell was suspended, and over the same was a small, tapering spire, and surmounting that was the rooster." In a recent interview, Mr. Bailey informed the writer that this description was based on what purported to be a wood cut of the edifice, seen by him in a collection of the antiquarian relics of Dutchess County, which was on exhibition in Poughkeepsie some forty years ago. Of the ultimate fate of the first edifice we have no certain knowledge. There is record of its repair in 1750. One of the deeds above quoted shows that it was standing in 1756. An entry in the records, dated February 15, 1760, speaks of its walls as fallen, but says nothing of the cause or manner of their fall.

### Second Edifice. 1760?–1822.

The entry just referred to, and dated February 15, 1760, informs us that the consistory had resolved to build another House of the Lord, and called on the congregation to subscribe for its erection.

The consistory appointed, as the builders of the new edifice, Boudewyn Lacounte, Elias Van Benschoten,

---

* 1 pr hengelses en slootje voor de Justeses Stoel 6–0.

Leonard Van Kleeck, and James Livingston, with instructions to look to the consistory for money, to receive estimates from the consistory how far they should proceed in the building from time to time, and to render account to the consistory every three months. It was also stipulated that the pews should be given out by the casting of lots, and that every subscriber should have credit for the sum subscribed on the cost of his pew.

The sums subscribed range from ten shillings to twelve pounds.

The records do not enable us to determine when this second edifice was completed. It was built on a lot on the north side of Main street, (then called East Lane,) conveyed by Gale Yelverton by a deed dated October 25, 1760.

Its location is clearly shown on a map of the homestead of Baltus Van Kleeck, which was made by Henry Livingston in May, 1800, and is in the Records of the Office of the County Clerk. On this map the church is depicted as standing on the north side of Main street, (then called East street,) directly opposite to the east side of Market street, (then called the Stage Road or Main street.) There the grave stones still standing indicate the adjoining burial ground, and there, a few years ago, the remnants of the walls of the church could be distinctly traced. There are a few still living who worshipped in it, and it is described by them as built of stone, and standing some twenty or thirty yards back from the line of the street, and fronting south, towards Main street.

Of the interior of this edifice there is, in one of the church books, a plan, drawn by Dr. Livingston in 1782, of which a reduced copy is given on the following page.

The plan shows that on the ground floor there were three aisles and 36 pews, exclusive of the two reserved

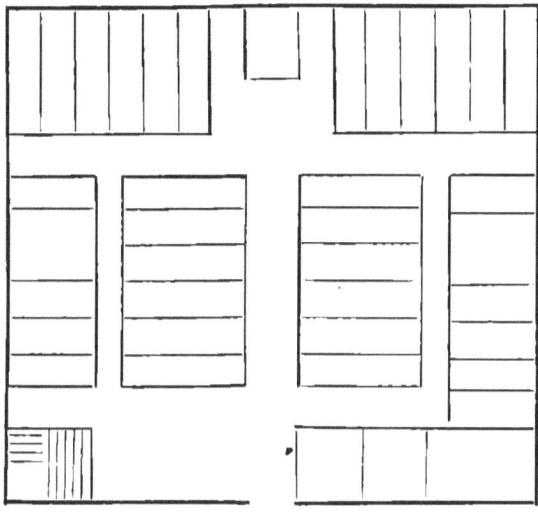

PLAN OF GROUND FLOOR AND GALLERY OF THE SECOND EDIFICE.

for the elders and deacons, and in the gallery, 18 pews, making 56 pews in all. Notes in the book, accompanying the plan, show that the pews contained 386 sittings, and that one of the pews was reserved for the "Magistrates."

This second edifice remained standing until 1822, when it was taken down, partly because it had become much out of repair, and partly because it was inadequate to the wants of the growing congregation.

### THIRD EDIFICE. 1822-1857.

On the 9th of January, 1822, the consistory earnestly recommended to the congregation to coöperate with them in building a new church, and requested the congregation to convene at the church on Monday, January 28th, for the purpose of taking the same into serious consideration.

The congregation met on the day appointed, and adopted the following resolutions:—

"*Resolved*, Unanimously, that this meeting agree that it is necessary to build a new church."

"*Resolved*, That this building committee consist of five persons."

"*Resolved*, That this committee consist of Robert Forrest, Abraham G. Storm, Henry A. Livingston, Joseph Parmalee, and John V. B. Varick."

It was also "*Resolved*, That the new church be located on the ground occupied by the Church now standing"; but at a subsequent meeting of the congregation, held two months later, (March 6th, 1822,) this resolution was reconsidered, and it was "*Resolved*, unanimously, that the New Church be erected on the east side of the parsonage lot."

In the two months intervening the old church must have been so far taken down as to be unfit for occupancy, for at the meeting held March 6, 1822, the consistory appointed a committee to make application to the supervisors for permission to use the court room "for the performing of public worship." The permission was granted, and without compensation.

The corner stone of the new edifice was laid May 6th, 1822, on which occasion an address was delivered by Rev. Cornelius C. Cuyler, who was then the pastor of the church.

At a meeting of consistory, held December 16, 1822, Col. Henry A. Livingston, in behalf of the building committee, reported that they had finally completed the new church and delivered the keys for the church;— whereupon the consistory, on the part of themselves and of the congregation, returned their most cordial thanks to the building committee "for the intelligent, un-wearied, and economical manner in which they had fulfilled their duties," and also to the supervisors of Dutchess county "for their kindness in granting to the congregation, free of rent or charge, the use of the court room for holding public worship."

The dedication took place December 24, 1822. The dedicatory sermon was preached by Rev. Dr. Cuyler, from the text, Exodus 20 : 24, "In all places where I record my name, I will come unto thee and I will bless thee." Both the sermon, and the address at the laying of the corner-stone, were published by request of the consistory, and copies of the pamphlet are still extant, bearing the imprint of P. Potter, Poughkeepsie, and the date, 1823.

This third edifice was of brick, stood where the present edifice stands, and resembled it much in size and architecture, except that the tower was in the center of the north end, instead of on the corner. This appears from a photograph, taken soon after the building was burned, and while the walls and tower were still standing.

As originally constructed, the pulpit had over it a sounding board, and was at the north end of the church, where, also, were the main entrances, so that late comers, on entering, faced the congregation.

In 1854 the interior was renovated and, as part of the renovation, a new pulpit was built, at the rear end of the church, and without the sounding board.

This edifice was occupied until Sunday, January 18, 1857, when it was destroyed by fire. The fire was discovered soon after the conclusion of the morning service. The following contemporaneous description is taken from the Weekly Eagle of January 24, 1857.

### FEARFUL FIRE.

On Sunday last, at about half past twelve o'clock, in the midst of a strong north wind and cold almost unendurable, our citizens were alarmed by the ring of an alarm of FIRE! As it is difficult to conceive of circumstances more fearful, there was a prompt rally from all quarters, when it was found that the roof of the First Dutch Reformed church was on fire. The firemen rushed to the rescue with their machines, but, as the hydrants were partially frozen, there was some delay before water could be obtained. In the meantime the flames were increasing with fearful rapidity in the roof of the church, fanned to a fury by the continuous blasts of wind.

When things were ready, one heroic fireman started up the long ladder planted on the east side, to take up the pipe to the roof, and thus play on the fire, but the cold was so intense it was doubtful if he could live there twenty minutes, and the hose was so slippery with ice it was impossible for the assistants to hold it up. So efforts to save the church had to be abandoned, and attention directed to the buildings around that were in great danger from the sparks of fire and burning shingles that were flying in all directions. Fortunately, all the roofs had more or less snow on them, which greatly aided in saving, so that they were soon rendered practically secure from the imminent danger that first threatened them.

As the fire progressed, the sight became fearful and sublime, if not terrible in the extreme. The entire roof, being composed of wood, cedar shingles laid on pine backing, sent up a mass of red flames, crackling and roaring in the wind, the extent and grandeur of which can hardly be imagined. But the greatest sight of all was the burning steeple. As the flames got hold of that they ascended with a rapidity that occupied but a few minutes until the red volume shot up beyond the ball and vane at the summit, presenting a fearful column of fire ascending far up towards the clouds. Above and below, all was flame and smoke for a short time; but soon the lower timbers that supported the steeple were burnt away, and then down came the lofty spire with a tremendous crash, carrying what remained of the burning roof with it down to the interior of the church. There the mass of burning material was so great that the entire space inside the walls which fortunately stood, seemed filled with flames until ten at night, although several streams of water were steadily poured in by the engines.

Although the loss in this instance falls on those well able to bear it, it was a sad sight to see the noble edifice burn. It had been thoroughly repaired and renovated but little more than a year ago, at an expense of between four and five thousand dollars, making the loss some $18,000. As the flames consumed the steeple, we almost fancied we could see the venerable Dr. Cuyler and his friends, and others, who were prominent among us in 1822, gathered around us to witness the destruction.

The old bell and clock perished with the rest. The insurance was but $6,000.

The firemen exerted themselves with a heroism that was worthy of all praise. Several of them were considerably injured by freezing.

The church had been on fire twice before, on the 4th of July, 1832,* and again on the 4th of July, 1843, in both of which instances it narrowly escaped destruction, the roof being fired by crackers thrown from the steeple.

As to the origin of the fire, we have no doubt it proceeded from a defect in the chimney.

---

* With respect to the fire of 1832, the universal and concurrent testimony of local survivors is, that on July 4th of that year, the son of the pastor, Dr. Cuyler, and some other lads, all brimfull of patriotism, contrived to get access to the steeple and gave vent to their patriotism by throwing fire crackers in all directions from the windows in the steeple. Some of the fire crackers lodged on the roof of the church, and thus the fire originated.

To add to the fearful events of the day, the alarms of fire were twice renewed, once between four and five P. M. and again at about eight in the evening. But it proved, in both cases, that the alarm was given in consequence of the fearful rekindling of the first fire, creating new dangers. When the last alarm was given, the storm had commenced with all its violence, so that, take all the events together, this day is one that will not be forgotten while the present generation of men lasts.

In the same paper it is said, in another column,—

Sunday was probably the coldest day known in this latitude for a century. At daylight, the thermometer stood at 18 degrees below zero, with a strong cutting wind from the north that was hardly endurable; at twelve at noon, it stood at 13 below; at three P. M., at 18 below; at five P. M., at 20 below, and all this in a clear day.

At between seven and eight, a violent snow storm set in from the northeast, with a stiff breeze, which soon increased to a furious gale or almost hurricane, which continued through the entire night and until near ten o'clock on Monday morning.

The writer has been informed, by some who were present, that on the morning of the fire, Rev. Charles A. Evans, a Presbyterian clergyman, was in the pulpit with the pastor, Rev. Dr. Mann, and had the chief conduct of the services. In his prayer was a petition that the church might become "a burning and a shining light" in the community, and not a few of the congregation, remembering the petition, expressed surprise that it should have been answered so soon, and in such an unexpected manner. The metal of the bell was recast into hand bells which were subsequently sold at a Ladies' Fair, held for the raising of funds for an organ in the new church. This was the first pipe organ owned by the church. The instrument used in the church that was burned was a small reed organ.

## FOURTH EDIFICE. 1857.

At the first meeting of the consistory after the fire, held January 23, 1857, communications were received from the Second Reformed church, the Presbyterian church, the Lafayette Street Baptist church, and Christ church, kindly tendering the use of their houses of worship to the congregation of the First Reformed church until the edifice of the latter should be rebuilt.

The consistory returned their cordial thanks to each of the said churches for their warm sympathy, and, after some deliberation, it was unanimously resolved that the invitation of the Second Reformed church be accepted. It was furthermore resolved that a new church shall be built on the old lot.

The corner-stone of the new edifice was laid August 25, 1857, with appropriate ceremony, and addresses by Rev. Samuel A. Van Vranken, D.D., and Rev. Cornelius Van Cleef, D.D.

In the corner-stone were deposited the three plates taken from the corner-stone of the old church, erected in 1822, and bearing the following inscriptions:

*1st Plate.*—Names of the persons who compose the consistory of the Reformed Dutch church, Poughkeepsie, April, 1822:

| ELDERS. | DEACONS. |
| --- | --- |
| Robert Forrest, | Peter A. Scriver, |
| Henry Barnes, | Joseph Parmalee, |
| Simeon De Groff, | George Bloom, |
| William Bell, | Frederic Phelps, |
| John V. B. Varick, | Abraham Ver Valen, |
| Hendrick Wiltsie. | Peter Pells. |

Rev. C. C. Cuyler.

*2nd Plate.*—Rev. C. C. Cuyler, born 15th February, 1783, ordained and installed 2nd January, 1809. This was deposited May 6th, 1822.

*3rd Plate.*—Names of the committee chosen by the congregation of the Dutch church to build a house for the worship of God:

Poughkeepsie, April, 1822.

100                           *History.*

COMMITTEE.

Robert Forrest, John V. B. Varick, Joseph Parmalee, Henry A. Livingston and Abraham G. Storm.

There were also deposited plates prepared for the occasion, and other articles as follows :

*1st Plate.*—Rev. C. C. Cuyler, D.D., dismissed December 17, 1833.

Rev. Samuel A. Van Vranken, D.D., installed September, 1834 ; dismissed December 15, 1837.

Rev. Alexander M. Mann, D.D., installed May, 1838 ; dismissed June 17, 1857.

*2nd Plate.*—Consistory of the First Reformed Dutch church :

| ELDERS. | DEACONS. |
|---|---|
| Cornelius Westervelt, | Daniel R. Thompson, |
| William Broas, | Elvy Deyo, |
| Henry D. Varick, | William Simmons, |
| Herman J. Jewitt. | J. C. McNeil, |
|  | John Van Keuren, |
|  | David B. Lent, Jr. |

*3rd Plate.*—Building committee :

| George Innis, | Herman J. Jewitt, |
|---|---|
| William Simmons, | Henry D. Varick, |
| David C. Foster, | William Broas, |
| Charles Carman, | James H. Warner. |

Architect—L. A. Gouch.
Builder—Samuel W. Hester.

June 1, 1857.

Map of the village of Poughkeepsie.
Poughkeepsie City Directory, 1856–57.
Poughkeepsie Eagle, January 24, 1857, containing an account of the destruction of the old church by fire.
Poughkeepsie Telegraph, August 25, 1857.
Daily City Press, August 25, 1857.
Poughkeepsie Eagle, August 22, 1857.
Poughkeepsie Examiner, August 27, 1857.
Dutchess County Times (Fishkill), August 22, 1857.
Ulster County Gazette, January 4, 1800.
Christian Intelligencer, August 13, and 20, 1857.

## Parsonages.

By-Laws, Rules and Regulations of Poughkeepsie Rural Cemetery.
Charter, Ordinances and By-Laws of the City of Poughkeepsie, 1854.
A sealed deposit by George Van Kleeck.
General Synod's Report on Foreign Mission, adopted June, 1857, with an appeal to the churches.
Specifications for the building of this church.

The church was dedicated on Tuesday, September 7, 1858. The sermon was preached by Rev. George W. Bethune, D.D., then the pastor of the church on Brooklyn Heights, and the other services were conducted by Rev. C. Van Cleef, D.D., Rev. C. S. Hageman, D. D., and Rev. J. R. Berry, D.D. The Rev. George M. McEckron was installed as pastor on the evening of the same day. The edifice thus dedicated is the one which is still standing and in use by the congregation. As originally built, it was adorned with a lofty spire, but in 1878 the spire was pronounced unsafe by reason of the decay of some of its frame-work, and was consequently taken down. In 1887 the roof and other portions of the exterior were repaired and the interior was renovated.

### PARSONAGES.

#### First Parsonage, 1732–1790.

When the united congregations of Poughkeepsie and Fishkill sent to Holland their first call for a minister (April 13, 1730), the church edifice in Poughkeepsie had already been erected and in use for about eight years. In neither place, however, was there a parsonage. Therefore in the call was inserted this promise to his Reverence : "He shall reside either in Poughkeepsie, or in Fishkill, or there-about, as shall be found most fit and to his best satisfaction, and in such place both congregations shall, at the first opportunity, build for him a suitable dwelling, and from time to time shall keep it in good repair."

On the 4th of October, 1731, four days after the arrival in Poughkeepsie of the first minister, Cornelius Van Schie, the two consistories held a joint meeting in Poughkeepsie, and resolved: "Whenever Dominie Van Schie shall have chosen to reside at Poughkeepsie or at the Fishkill, there, where he chooses to live, both congregations together, (each bearing half of the expense,) shall buy six acres, build a house, and make a garden, and plant an orchard, in accordance with the stipulations on these points made in the power of attorney call."

Dominie Van Schie selected Poughkeepsie as his place of residence, and there, in fulfillment of their promise, the two congregations bought the land on part of which the present church edifice and parsonage stand, and on it built the first parsonage. It was probably finished in 1732. In a call sent to Holland, and dated April 20, 1734, it is described as "A new and suitable residence, forty-five feet long and twenty-seven broad, having three rooms, and a study upstairs, a large cellar under the house, a well with good water, a garden, and an orchard planted with 100 fruit trees."

It was occupied by Dominie Van Schie until his departure to Albany in 1733. Then came an interval of twelve years during which the church was without a pastor, and the records show that for some, and possibly for all, of these years, the parsonage was rented to one John Constable at three pounds a year, from which, however, was to be deducted the amount expended by Constable in keeping the house in repair.*

---

\* Juni der eerste dagh Annog domini een duisent seven hondert en vertigh en een, dan heb ick Johannis van Kleek gherecent met John Con-

*Parsonages.*

On the arrival of Dominie Meynema, in 1745, it was occupied by him; and, in the calls to his successors, Van Nist and Schoonmaker, it is designated as "the house in which Dominie Meynema had lived."

Subsequent to the departure of Mr. Schoonmaker, in 1774, no mention of the first parsonage has been discovered in the records. It probably stood until about 1790. Neither do the records give any clear information concerning its precise location on the parsonage lot and the materials of which it was built; with the exception

---

stable van de huer van dominis huis en Besids de onkosten blift Constable Schuldigh de somma van . . . . . . . £1-17-0

*Translation.*—June, the first day, Anno Domini one thousand seven hundred and forty-one, have I, Johannes Van Kleek, reckoned with John Constable for the rent of the Dominie's house and besides the charges, Constable still owes the sum of . . . . . . . . £1-17-0

On the page opposite to the above entry is the following:

De huer van et huis is drie pont jaers.

Juni de 8 dagh, Annog 1741, dan broght John Constable zyn Rekenen wat hy van oncosten had tegen et huis.

| | |
|---|---|
| to 6 Busals Callick @ 4/6 an riye @ 6 p, | £0-5-0 |
| to william herris for majen of an oven, | 0-10-0 |
| an ecten en drenken @ 2/6, . . . | 0-2-6 |
| an Frans Filkin zyn niger voor 2 dagen, . | 0-4-0 |
| an cost nog @ 1/ . . . . . | 0-1-0 |
| an oven voren betalt @ 6 p., . | 0-0-6 |
| | £1-3-0 |

*Translation.*—The rent of the house is three pounds a year.

June 8, 1741. Then John Constable brought his account of his charges against the house.

| | |
|---|---|
| To 6 bushels lime 4/6 and cartage /6, . | £0-5-0 |
| To William Harris for making an oven, . | 0-10-0 |
| To eating and drinking 2/6 . . . | 0-2-6 |
| To Frans Filkin for his negro 2 days, | 0-4-0 |
| To sundries 1/- . . . . . | 0-1-0 |
| To paid before on oven /6, . | 0-0-6 |
| | £1-3-0 |

that there is in existence a paper which shows that, when the second parsonage was built, a new cellar was dug, from which it must be inferred that the location of the second parsonage, (which was also that of the third,) was different from that of the first. This inference is corroborated by a map in the office of the Secretary of State in Albany, entitled "Map of the lands of Poughkeepsie as they are held under the patent of Saunders and Heermance, surveyed pursuant to a warrant dated January 23, 1770." On this map the parsonage is represented as situated on the south side of what is now Main street and a short distance back from the line of the street. In other words, its location is represented as having been a little south of that of the present parsonage.

## SECOND PARSONAGE, 1794–1844.

About 1774 the union of the two churches of Poughkeepsie and Fishkill was dissolved by mutual consent. The original agreement (October 4, 1731) had been that if such dissolution should ever take place, then, inasmuch as the glebe and parsonage were the joint property of both congregations, the congregation retaining them in sole possession should pay to the other the just half of their appraised value. The just half was paid by the congregation of Poughkeepsie to the congregation of Fishkill, as appears from a paper in possession of the church, and headed, "An abstract from the subscription list of the subscribers towards purchasing half of the glebe or parsonage in Poughkeepsie from the congregation of Fishkill, dated June 8th, 1790."

The congregation of Poughkeepsie, having thus acquired sole possession of the glebe, began to build upon it a new parsonage in 1791, and finished it not later than 1794. In evidence of this there are:

First—A contract for work to be done on the "parrich house" dated August 27, 1791.*

Second—A bill headed "Minister's House Dr. to Myndert Van Kleeck," amounting to 81 pounds, 7 shillings and 7 pence, for labor and building materials, and running through the years 1791-3, and ending May 11, 1794.†

Third—A paper dated May 10, 1793, headed "An abstract from the subscription list for building the minister's house belonging to the Dutch church of Poughkeepsie."

Fourth—A subscription list dated April 7, 1794, for "the completing of the parsonage house, and the improvement of the lot whereon it stands.

Fifth—The minutes of the consistory from 1792 to the end of 1793, in which frequent mention is made of the parsonage as in process of construction. This was during the pastorate of Rev. Andrew Gray.

In the call made to his successor, Rev. Cornelius Brower, February 1, 1794, the use of the parsonage house is offered as one of the inducements to acceptance. At that date, therefore, it was finished and ready for occupancy. This second parsonage is remembered by not a few still living, for it stood until 1844.

It is described by Dr. Mann, who lived in it during the last seven years of its existence, as being, at that time, a very old and uncouth structure, built of wood, with low ceilings, standing precisely on the location of the

---

* 1791, August 27. I Isaac Romine Agreaed with peter Tappen for the parrich house the Seler To Be 44 By 21 feet 2 Store hye, 1 Shimble at Ech End Each one to Be Dubeld Smok, 2 Romes Below and a gang Below aBove the same to B Seld and plasterd. I am to have, . . . £30 – 0 – 0 and find my Self.

† The first and last items of this bill are :
Aug. 11, 1791. To 2 Gallons of Rum for digging the Seller @ 6/6,   13–0
May 11, 1794. To 1 pair Hinges pr Swartwot for . . . .   7–0

present parsonage, but with the gable end to the street, having its front entrance on the east towards the church, and a hall running from east to west, and an entrance to the yard, from the street, of seven or eight stone steps.

### THIRD PARSONAGE, 1844.

At a meeting of consistory, held April 15, 1844, there was presented a petition, signed by 113 names, requesting that the consistory take into consideration the expediency, propriety, and necessity of building a new parsonage. An adjourned meeting of consistory was held on the next day, for the purpose of considering the petition, and it was then

"*Resolved*, that the consistory deem it necessary, either to erect a new parsonage, or to repair and refit the present one; but the consistory do not feel themselves warranted in assuming the responsibility of doing either, until they have a free expression of the members of the congregation."

"*Resolved*, that a meeting of the male members of the church be called on Monday next, at 10 o'clock A. M., in the lecture room, for the purpose of obtaining their views with respect to a new parsonage."

At the meeting of the male members of the congregation thus called, and held at the time appointed, (April 15, 1844,) it was "*Resolved*, that, in the opinion of this meeting, a new parsonage, suitable for the accommodation of our pastor and his family, is absolutely necessary, and ought to be erected as speedily as possible."

On May 21, 1844, proposals were presented, and on the day following it was "*Resolved*, that the proposal of Mr. Henry Tittamer, of twenty-nine hundred and fifty dollars for building a parsonage house, agreeably to the plan and specifications estimated upon, (it being the lowest estimate handed in,) be accepted; and that the building committee be authorized to enter into a contract with him to do the work, as therein set forth and specified, for the above amount."

The building committee appointed consisted of five members; three from the congregation, and two from the consistory. The three from the congregation were John B. Forbus, David H. Barnes, and James H. Allen. The two from the consistory were Isaac H. Coller, and David C. Foster.

Just six months after their appointment, (Nov. 22, 1844,) this committee met at the parsonage house, then completed, and unanimously agreed to receive said house, and pay for the same, agreeably to contract, and their report to that effect was presented to the consistory and approved December 2, 1844.

The house thus received is the brick parsonage now standing on Main Street west of the church.

## LANGUAGE.

At the time of the organization of the church the mother tongue of nearly all the inhabitants of the region was the Dutch, and therefore in that language the first ministers preached, and the earliest records of the church were written. But, from the final end of Dutch rule, and the beginning of English supremacy in 1674, the language of the law and the government had been the English, and there is evidence that, even in the earliest years of the existence of the church, at least some of its members were not unacquainted with that language. Some of the earliest of the receipts preserved are in English, and there is a record in English of at least one instance of English preaching, as far back as 1740.*

---

* Ano 1740. Sunday ye 19 of October, Mr. Robertson an English prespeterian minister preched and Mr. Abraham De Graeff and I Colected from ye people and In ye Contribution we gott in all the sum of sixteen shillings & ½ penny and we offered it to Mr. Robertson but he refused it.

The records, however, are almost exclusively in Dutch until the ministry of Dr. Livingston, which began in 1781, and ended in 1783. Then, for the first time, the English begins to appear to any noticeable extent, and, so far as the records are concerned, with the close of his ministry the Dutch totally disappears. A new book of records was begun by his successor, Mr. Gray, and of this book the contents are exclusively in English, with the exception of the title, which is in Latin.

With respect to the change of language in public worship, the heading of the subscription paper for the calling of Rev. Andrew Gray shows that preaching in Dutch and English was desired and stipulated for in 1790.* The following also appears in the minutes of consistory, June 5, 1793:

"The consistory having taken into consideration the great declension of the Dutch Language, and conceiving that, by continuing the service in that Language so frequently as heretofore observed, would not only be injurious to the edification of the Congregation at large, but tend rather to its decrease than growth."

"The Consistory therefore direct, that henceforward the Service be performed in the Dutch Language every third Lord's Day in the forenoon, and service at all other time in the English Tongue."

From the action thus taken, it is evident that even then, the English language had been for some years encroaching upon and displacing the Dutch. In the call which was extended to Mr. Brouwer, less than one year afterward (February 3, 1794,) there is no mention whatever of the Dutch Language, and it is stipulated that he is to "Preach twice every Lord's Day in the Church in Poughkeepsie in the English Language"; from which it may be inferred that, in the brief intervening period, the displacement had become substantially complete.

---

* See page 69.

## FORMATION OF THE SECOND REFORMED CHURCH.
### 1847.

The Second Reformed church was organized chiefly by members dismissed from the First Reformed church for that purpose.

If was at first proposed that the two churches should be Collegiate; that is, should constitute one church and ecclesiastical corporation, having one consistory, but with two congregations, and worshipping in two edifices.

As the project matured this proposal was abandoned, and it was decided that the two churches should be separate organizations. The history as contained in the records of the First Reformed church, is substantially as follows :

At a meeting of the consistory held August 2, 1847, it was "*Resolved*, that in the opinion of this consistory, it is expedient now to make an effort towards building a new church."

At the same meeting a committee was appointed "to confer with members of the church and congregation, and others who are friendly to the object of building a Second Reformed Dutch church, and obtain their views and feelings on the subject, and that the said committee open a subscription for the purpose of ascertaining how much money can be raised for said purpose."

The committee reported, August 26, 1847, that they had secured $7,150 ; whereupon it was "*Resolved*, that consistory, while they feel desirous of promoting the building of a new church, do not feel willing to take the responsibility of building a Collegiate church without the advice of the congregation."

At a meeting of the congregation, duly called and held August 31st, 1847, it was "*Resolved*, that in the opinion of this congregation, it is expedient and proper for the consistory to adopt the necessary measures for the immediate erection of a Collegiate church."

Notwithstanding this expression of opinion by the congregation, at the next meeting of the consistory (September 5, 1847), a resolution offered, "That in the judgment of this consistory it is expedient to build a Collegiate church," was decided in the negative. At the same meeting a committee was appointed to "ascertain whether consistory have a right to give to a new Reformed Dutch church any part of the property of this church, and also to confer with the subscribers for pews in the new church, to ascertain whether they, and which of them, will organize and build a new Reformed Dutch church."

After hearing the reports of the committee, the consistory, September 16, 1847, resolved to convey the real estate lying west of the parsonage lot, "in trust, to use the same towards the building of a Second Reformed Dutch church in the village of Poughkeepsie, and for the support and maintenance of public worship therein, provided consistory have a legal right so to do." A committee was also appointed to make application to the Supreme Court for power to convey the said real estate.

It was also resolved, that in case the court should decide that consistory had no legal right to convey, then "Consistory will lease the property for a term of nine hundred and ninety-nine years, at one dollar per year, to said new church, when duly organized and incorporated and the house of worship completed."

The records in the office of the county clerk show that the property was conveyed November 10, 1847, under an order from the Supreme Court, and on condition that a church building should be erected within two years.

At the meeting of consistory, November 2, 1847, Elder C. P. Adriance tendered his resignation of office, "with a

## Formation of the Second Reformed Church. 1847. 111

view of connecting himself as an elder to build up a Second Reformed Dutch church in this village," and his resignation was accepted, with expressions of mingled regret for his departure, and approval of the step he had taken. At the same meeting, Charles P. Adriance, Abraham G. Storm, Joseph H. Jackson, James W. Bogardus, Caspar D. Smith and Albert Brett were dismissed, "for the purpose of enabling them to unite with others in the formation of the Second Reformed Dutch church in Poughkeepsie."

At a special meeting of Classis, held in the church of Poughkeepsie on the evening of the same day, the action, as recorded in the minutes of Classis, was as follows:

The object of the meeting was stated by Rev. A. M. Mann, and an application presented for the organization of a Second Reformed Dutch church in the village of Poughkeepsie. The committee, consisting of Nathan Jewett, Tunis Brinkerhoff, and Joseph H. Jackson, who had been previously appointed by the congregation to make arrangement for securing this organization, presented the names of Abraham G. Storms, Charles P. Adriance, Tunis Brinkerhoff and Joseph H. Jackson for elders, and James W. Bogardus, Caspar D. Smith, Albert Brett, and John P. Flagler for deacons, and requested that they be organized into a church as early as practicable. Whereupon, after receiving their certificates of dismission, Classis

*Resolved*, That the request be granted, and that we immediately proceed to effect the organization.

*Resolved*, That Rev. F. M. Kip preach the sermon, Rev. A. Elmendorf read the form prescribed for ordaining elders and deacons, and that the Rev. A. M. Mann address the officers when ordained. All of which was attended to in accordance with the above resolution.

The elders and deacons, having been thus ordained, were in a position to receive members from other churches, and the report of the First church to the Classis, April 5, 1850, shows that, in the preceding year, twenty-seven members had been dismissed from the First church, in order that they might connect themselves with the Second church.

Thus the Second Church was established as a separate organization, but although separate organizations, the two churches have ever been closely united, not only by the ties of denominational communion, but also by those of fervent brotherly love.

## MISCELLANEA.

### Armen Kas and Armen Gelt.

In the older records frequent mention is made of the "Armen Kas," which means, literally, the "Chest of the Poor." There are, however, no entries showing that money was paid out of it for the poor; and probably there was no need of such payment, for, although nearly all the people were in circumstances more or less straitened, they were able to support themselves, and self respect restrained even the poorest from seeking pecuniary aid from the church. Hence the Armen Kas came to be virtually the treasury of the church, and in that sense the term occurs constantly in the records. So, in like manner, the collections taken up from Sunday to Sunday are called the "Armen Gelt," signifying, literally, "Money for the Poor," but, nevertheless, were evidently turned, for the most part, into the general treasury of the church. There is still preserved a little book containing the account of the "Armen Gelt," or collections, from 1739 to 1741, and the following extracts from it are interesting, as showing the financial condition of the people, and the manner of holding public service.

## Miscellanea.

During these years the church was without a pastor, and it will be observed that it was only occasionally that the people had the privilege of hearing a sermon from a neighboring minister, and that, generally, the service was conducted by a Voorlezer (Fore Reader) chosen from among themselves.

Anno. 1739, May de 31.—In presenties van de Kerickeraden Van Pockepsinck mett Namen Johannes Van Kleeck, ouderling, Elias Van Beenschoten onderling, Henry Vanderburgh Diakon, Johannes Tappen Diakon, Abraham De Graff Diakon, heben wy De Kass Geteld En Vonden Dare In de Some Van dree pont In Coper Geldt En Twe Schelings En Sixpence.
£ 3 - 2 - 6
An Sewant De Some van Darteen Schellingen en
Negen Pence. . . . . . . . 0-13-9

*Translation.*—In presence of the consistory of Poughkeepsie, named Johannes Van Kleeck, elder; Elias Van Beenschoten, elder; Henry Vanderburgh, deacon; Johannes Tappen, deacon; Abraham De Graff, deacon; we have counted the chest, and found therein the sum of three pounds in copper money, and two shillings and sixpence. . . £ 3 - 2 - 6
In Sewant (wampum) the sum of thirteen shillings
and nine pence. . . . . . . 0 - 13 - 9

Ano. 1739, Augustus de 5.—Sondagh en morghen yonge Bartolomeus Hoogeboom Versoght Voor Veur te Lassen, en ben Ick Rontgegan en Kreegh en het Sackie Tweentig pence half penny. . . . . . . . . 0 - 1 - 8½

*Translation.*—1739, August 5. Sunday morning, young Bartolomeus Hoogeboom requested to act as Voorlezer, and I went around and took in the bag twenty pence halfpenny.
0 - 1 - 8½

Ano. 1739, Augustus de 19.—Sondagh en morgen Mr. Vander Lyn Las Voor; ben Ick om gegan en Kreeg Twe Schellengs en Twe pennys en Twe Stuffers. 0 - 2 - 2

*Translation.*—1739, August 19. Sunday morning, Mr. Vanderlyn Voorlezer; I went about and took two shillings and two pennies and two stivers. . . . . . 0 - 2 - 2

Ano. 1739, September de 9. Sondagh en morghen Mr. Vander Lyn Las Voor ben Ick om gegan en Kreeg Drie Schellingen en five penns en en half penny. . . . . 0 - 3 - 5¼

*Translation.*—1739, September 9. Sunday morning, Mr. Vander Lyn Voorlezer, I went about and took three shillings and five pennies and one half penny. . . . 0 – 3 – 5½

Ano. 1739, October de 14. Sondagh en morgen Johannes Rynders Las Voor ben Ick om gegan en Kreeg En Schelige en Twe pence half penny en 3 wetis. . . . . 0–1–2½

*Translation.*—1739, October 14. Sunday morning, Johannes Rynders Voorlezer, I went about and took one shilling and two pence half penny and 3 (white wampum beads ?) 0 – 1 – 2½

Ano. 1739, November 4. Sondagh en morgen Johannes Rynders Las Voor ben Ick om gegan en Kreeg En Schelige en Drie pence half penny en seven wetyes. . . 0 – 1 – 3½

*Translation.*—1739, November 4. Sunday morning, Johannis Rynders Voorlezer, I went about and took one shilling and three pence half penny and seven (white wampum beads ?) 0 – 1 – 3½

Ano. 1739, December de 2. Sondagh Johannes Vermanus Van Basten predichte gang Ick om en Kreeg five Schelinge in pennys en Ses en Twentigh half pennys en wy gaven de fife Schellingen an Domine Van Basten. . . . 0 – 1 – 1

*Translation.*—1739, December 2. Sunday Johannes Vermanus Van Basten preached. I went about and took five shillings in pennies, and six and twenty half pennies, and we gave the five shillings to Domine Van Basten. . . 0 – 1 – 1

Ano. 1739, December 23. Student Van Basten predichten. Ben Ick om gegan En Kreegh Twe Schelingen en Negen pence en fifteen half pennys, maken samen De Soma Van Drie Schellingen En Drie pence halfpenny. . . 0 – 3 – 3½

*Translation.*—1739, December 23. Student Van Basten preached. I went around and took two shillings and nine pence and fifteen half pennies, the same making the sum of three shillings and three pence half penny. . . 0 – 3 – 3½

Ano. 1740, March ye 2. Ben Ick om gegan en Kregh fourteen pence halfpenny. . . . . . 0 – 1 – 2½

*Translation.*—1740, March 2. I went about and took fourteen pence halfpenny. . . . . . 0 – 1 – 2½

Anno, 1740, May ye 8. Domine Vass Boout predicase op Dondedag. Ben Ick om gegan en Kreegh five Schelengen en Veerpence. . . . . . . . 0 – 5 – 4

*Translation.*—1740, May 8. Dominie Vas preached a penitential sermon (Preparatory lecture) on Thursday. I went about and took five shillings and four pence. . 0 – 5 – 4

## Miscellanea. 115

The foregoing extracts from August 5, 1739, to May 8, 1740, are in the order in which they occur in the Armen Gelt book, and are all that are in the book for that period. The Record of Baptisms (in another book) shows that on the day following the penitential sermon above mentioned, (May 9, 1750,) Domine Vas baptized twenty-six children. After that date there is in the Armen Gelt book no mention of preaching again until October 8, 1740, when the following occurs :

Ano. 1740, October ye 8. Domine Vas predickte En wy Kereck Raden betalde hem fiftigh Schellingen Voor Syn dienst En Dare Resterde Ses Schellingen en Five pennys half pennys.
0 – 6 – 2¼

*Translation.*—1740, October 8. Domine Vas preached, and we, the consistory, paid him fifty shillings for his service, and there remained six shillings and two pence half penny. 0 – 6 – 2¼

Correspondingly, in the Record of Baptisms, there are no entries again until October 8, 1740, when nine children were baptised. It must be inferred that during the five months intervening, no neighboring minister preached in the Church, and the only services were those conducted by the Voorlezer.

### PALLS.

The records show that, soon after its organization, the the church owned two palls, one large, (Dood Kleed,) for grown persons, and one small, (Kleine Dood Kleed,) for children, and that the church was paid for their use at funerals. The following are some of the entries bearing on this subject :

DUTCHESS COUNTY, June ye 4th, Ano. 1739.

Then Received from Henry Vanderburgh, Decon of the Church of Pockepsinck, the Sum of Twelve Shillings, and Thirty Two Shillings and Six pence formerly Received of Hendrick pells, which is In full for a Black Cloath ; to Bury the Dead ; I Say Received In full per me.

FRAˢ FILKINS.

In 1741 there is a charge of one shilling and sixpence for the use of the little pall, (cline clet,) and from 1741 to 1747 there are several charges of three shillings for the use of the large pall. Mr. Jonathan Pearson, in his history of the church in Schenectady, says that, in that church, the charge for the use of the large pall was three shillings, and for the use of the little pall, one shilling and sixpence. The foregoing citations show that the charges in Poughkeepsie were the same, and it may be inferred that these were the customary charges throughout an extensive region.

### Subscribers for Call to Holland.

It has already been stated that the call, which was sent to Holland in 1744, was accompanied by a sum of money, for the payment of the minister's passage to this country. It appears, from various bills and receipts, that this money was advanced by Mr. Joris Brinkerhoff, of New York, and was repaid in small installments, and that the last installment was not paid until 1753.

Meanwhile efforts were in progress to procure the money, as appears from the following :

Augt den 7 dagh Anno 1745, dan hebben wey de name van de Lest van die die Beloft hebben an et beroep dat na hollandt is voor een domini.

*Translation.*—Aug. 7, 1745, then have we the names of the list of those who have promised for the call to Holland for a minister.

Inasmuch as most of the earlier records of the county were destroyed in the burning of the Court House, in 1785, the list of subscribers is here given, as being probably one of the most complete lists now extant, of the heads of families then residing in this portion of the county. It is as follows :

## Miscellanea. 117

| | £ | s | d | | £ | s | d |
|---|---|---|---|---|---|---|---|
| Lewis Dubois, | 1 | 0 | 0 | Johannis Palmetir, | 0 | 3 | 0 |
| Geisbort Pele, | 0 | 16 | 0 | Frances Hegeman, | 0 | 5 | 6 |
| William Sifer, | 0 | 10 | 0 | Hendrick Hegeman, | 0 | 5 | 0 |
| Markus Van Boml, | 0 | 10 | 0 | Barent Band, | 0 | 3 | 0 |
| Jacobus V Boml, | 0 | 5 | 0 | Magil Pels, | 0 | 5 | 0 |
| Samuel Mettus, | 0 | 6 | 0 | Mosas Degraef, | 0 | 8 | 0 |
| Jeams Luckey, | 0 | 5 | 0 | Baltus Kep, | 0 | 3 | 0 |
| Cristopel Van Boml, | 0 | 9 | 0 | Lendert Lewis, | 0 | 3 | 0 |
| Francis Jacobs, | 0 | 3 | 0 | Cornelus V d bogert, | 0 | 4 | 0 |
| Piter Lassing, | 0 | 2 | 0 | Lawerens Gerbrands, | 0 | 12 | 0 |
| Dollif Swartwout, | 0 | 10 | 0 | Anthony Jelverton, | 0 | 4 | 0 |
| Thomas Sanders, | 0 | 4 | 0 | John Gay, | 0 | 4 | 0 |
| Henry Wilson, | 0 | 8 | 0 | Boudewin Lakounta, | 0 | 12 | 0 |
| William V Vlet, | 0 | 10 | 0 | John Tenbrock, | 0 | 16 | 0 |
| Matthew Van Kurren, | 0 | 10 | 0 | Hendrick Osterom, | 0 | 8 | 0 |
| John Littel, | 0 | 2 | 0 | Mindert V d bogert, | 0 | 9 | 0 |
| Cornelus Arsen, | 0 | 6 | 0 | JacobusV d bogert, Jun., | 0 | 3 | 0 |
| Johanis V Benthussen, | 0 | 8 | 0 | Piter Van debogert, | 0 | 3 | 0 |
| Henry Levingston, | 0 | 10 | 0 | Nensi Wittenton, | 0 | 3 | 0 |
| John Canklen, | 0 | 13 | 0 | Ellixzander Grigx, | 0 | 6 | 0 |
| Piter Windevort, | 0 | 4 | 0 | Joris Cock, | 0 | 2 | 6 |
| Abraham Freer, Jun., | 0 | 10 | 0 | Johnis Bogert. | 0 | 4 | 0 |
| JacobusVandenBogert, | 0 | 15 | 0 | Jacob Low, | 0 | 8 | 0 |
| Borth : Noxon, | 0 | 5 | 0 | Elias V Bontschoten, | | | |
| John Mecferling, | 0 | 6 | 0 | Jun., | 0 | 3 | 0 |
| Jeams Mecgorog, | 0 | 3 | 0 | Elias Van Bontschoten, | 0 | 15 | 0 |
| Jeams Lechal, | 0 | 6 | 0 | Francis Laroy, | 0 | 10 | 0 |
| Piter Van Kleck, | 0 | 8 | 0 | Tunnis Van Vlit, | 0 | 7 | 0 |
| Johannis Swartwont, | 0 | 8 | 0 | Bengamen Pele, | 0 | 2 | 0 |
| Hannis Van Kleeck, | 0 | 15 | 0 | Anderis Pele, | 0 | 2 | 0 |
| Jacobus Van Kleeck, | 0 | 4 | 0 | Piter V d burgh, | 0 | 2 | 0 |
| Simon Freer, | 0 | 16 | 0 | John Van den burgh, | 0 | 4 | 0 |
| Mateues Kep, | 0 | 5 | 0 | Augustinus Turck, | 0 | 8 | 0 |
| Henry Vandrburgh, | 0 | 16 | 0 | Joseph Herris, | 0 | 6 | 0 |
| Rechard Vandrburgh, | 0 | 8 | 0 | Johannis Tapin, | 1 | 0 | 0 |
| Barnardus Swartwout, | 0 | 9 | 0 | Isack Cromel, | 0 | 3 | 0 |
| Januatie Doyo, | 0 | 1 | 6 | Henry V d burgh, Jun., | 0 | 6 | 0 |
| Magil Palmetie, Jun., | 0 | 8 | 0 | Johannis Lewis, | 0 | 6 | 0 |
| Jeams Aggemody, | 0 | 6 | 0 | Robert Kidny, | 0 | 8 | 0 |
| Piter Palmetir, | 0 | 13 | 0 | Elisabet Kep, | 0 | 2 | 0 |
| Mindert Palmetir, | 0 | 3 | 0 | Hendrick Pels, | 0 | 8 | 0 |
| Piter Palmetir, Jun., | 0 | 3 | 0 | Evert Pels, | 0 | 10 | 0 |
| Jacobus Palmetir, | 0 | 3 | 0 | Francis Filkin, | 1 | 0 | 0 |

*History.*

|  | £ | s | d |  | £ | s | d |
|---|---|---|---|---|---|---|---|
| John Mexfild, | 0 | 6 | 0 | Denie Relye, | 0 | 3 | 0 |
| Thomas Lewis, | 0 | 6 | 0 | Joseph Gonsallusdock, | 0 | 5 | 0 |
| John d Graef, | 0 | 3 | 0 | Zagharias Vlegelar, | 0 | 5 | 0 |
| Jacobus Stoutenburgh, | 0 | 12 | 0 | Barent Lewis, | 0 | 15 | 0 |
| John Emens, | 0 | 5 | 0 | Mosas Ver Veelen, | 0 | 12 | 0 |
| Barrent V Kleck, | 0 | 18 | 0 | Gidiyon Vr Veelen, | 0 | 6 | 0 |
| Lowerens V Kleck, | 1 | 0 | 0 | Johannis Ruger, | 0 | 12 | 0 |
| Arry V Vlet, | 0 | 10 | 0 | Ezegil Masten, | 0 | 12 | 0 |
| Swerris V Kleck, | 0 | 10 | 0 | Simon Pels, | 0 | 10 | 0 |
| Abraham de Graef, | 0 | 18 | 0 | Mannul Gonsallusdock, | 0 | 3 | 0 |
| Isack Hegeman, | 0 | 10 | 0 | Joseph Hegeman, | 0 | 8 | 0 |
| Baltus Van Kleck, | 0 | 11 | 0 | Isack Filkin, | 0 | 12 | 0 |
| Cornelus Vr Wiye, | 0 | 3 | 0 | Simon Vlegelar, | 0 | 8 | 0 |
| Abraham Swartwout, | 0 | 9 | 0 | Henry Filkin, | 0 | 10 | 0 |
| Abraham Provort, | 0 | 4 | 0 | Stipen Crego, | 0 | 5 | 0 |
| William Grigx, | 0 | 4 | 0 | Henry Smith, | 0 | 6 | 0 |
| Johannis Buis, Jun. | 0 | 3 | 0 | Isack Germon, | 0 | 3 | 0 |
| Gerret Daveds, | 0 | 4 | 0 | George Elsewort, Jun., | 0 | 5 | 0 |
| Jacob Van Wagene, | 0 | 8 | 0 | George Elsewort, | 0 | 10 | 0 |
| John Grin, | 0 | 2 | 0 | Hendrick Thomas, | 0 | 2 | 0 |
| Daved Daveds, | 0 | 4 | 0 | Art Masten, | 0 | 4 | 6 |
| Harmanis Rinderse, Jun., | 0 | 13 | 0 | Barent Kep, | 0 | 2 | 0 |
| Simon Laroy, | 0 | 10 | 0 | Cornelus Masten, | 0 | 5 | 0 |
| Harman Rinderse, | 0 | 3 | 0 | Mindert Vilen, | 0 | 11 | 0 |
| Matthaus Dubous, | 0 | 14 | 0 | William Herris, | 0 | 10 | 0 |
| Gidiyon dubois, | 0 | 8 | 0 | William Freer, | 0 | 6 | 0 |
| Jerimiya dubois, | 0 | 8 | 0 | William Smith, | 0 | 8 | 0 |
| Eferom dubois, | 0 | 6 | 0 | Arry Cool, | 0 | 6 | 0 |
| Johannis Rinderse, | 0 | 10 | 0 | Bortho : Crennel, | 0 | 10 | 0 |
| Jan Osterom, | 0 | 7 | 0 | John Laroy, | 0 | 8 | 0 |
| Rollif Ostrom, | 0 | 11 | 0 | Thomas Voos, | 0 | 9 | 0 |
| Daved Relye, | 0 | 3 | 0 | Elizabeth Lewis, | 0 | 8 | 0 |
| Gerret Van Wagene, | 0 | 4 | 0 | Piter Heiyer, | 0 | 6 | 0 |
| Nicklas Van Wagene, | 0 | 7 | 0 | Hendrick Kep, | 0 | 6 | 0 |
| Hendrick Lot, | 0 | 10 | 0 | Frans Cool, | 0 | 6 | 0 |
| Hendrick Hegeman, | 0 | 10 | 0 | Bengemen Bertlit, | 0 | 6 | 0 |
| Jan Hegeman, | 0 | 9 | 0 | Jacob Schouten, | 0 | 3 | 0 |
| Jacobes Schut, | 0 | 7 | 0 | Borth : Hogeboom, | 0 | 3 | 0 |
| Baltus Jos Van Kleck, | 0 | 7 | 0 | Jacob Dolsen, | 0 | 6 | 0 |
| Baltus Ls Van Kleck, | 0 | 6 | 0 | Abraham Dolsen, | 0 | 8 | 0 |
| Jan Meckinni, | 0 | 4 | 0 | Gaberel Werit, | 0 | 4 | 0 |
| Lendert Van Kleck, | 0 | 4 | 0 | Johannis Buis, | 0 | 8 | 0 |
|  |  |  |  | Hendrick Bertlit, | 0 | 5 | 0 |

## Miscellanea. 119

| | £ | s | d | | £ | s | d |
|---|---|---|---|---|---|---|---|
| Jacob Scherpenston, | 0 | 4 | 0 | John Van Dormaln, | 0 | 3 | 0 |
| Hendrick Boos, | 0 | 4 | 0 | Moses, son of Abraham | | | |
| Piter V Campen, | 0 | 6 | 0 | Degroff, | 0 | 5 | 0 |
| Jan Van Campen, | 0 | 6 | 0 | Cornelius Vealy, | 0 | 3 | 0 |
| Abraham fontin, | 0 | 5 | 0 | John Edwards, | 0 | 4 | 0 |
| Sander Brouwer, | 0 | 6 | 0 | Lawrence Delong, | 0 | 6 | 0 |
| Damen Palmetir, | 0 | 10 | 0 | Peter Laroy, | 0 | 5 | 0 |
| Piter Vilen, | 0 | 12 | 0 | Ragel Swartwout, | 0 | 5 | 0 |
| MosasBengemenFranks, | 0 | 5 | 9 | Phillip Harmensen, | 0 | 3 | 0 |
| Kasparis Westervelt, | 0 | 15 | 0 | Johannis Davitson, | 0 | 4 | 0 |
| Cornelius Osborn, | 0 | 5 | 0 | Jan Oasstrom, (son of | | | |
| Frans Hageman, | 0 | 5 | 0 | Hendrick), | 0 | 2 | 0 |
| Charles Doughty, | 0 | 5 | 0 | Myndert Vandebogart, | | | |
| Seimon Frayer, Jun$^r$, | 0 | 4 | 0 | (son of Frans), | 0 | 6 | 0 |
| Andres Suuck, | 0 | 3 | 0 | Petrus Low, | 0 | 2 | 0 |
| Cathenah Stenbergh, | 0 | 1 | 6 | | | | |

### First Things.

#### First Baptism.

The names of the first elders and deacons have already been given. On the day on which they were installed (October 10, 1716), the minister who installed them, Rev. Petrus Vas, of Kingston, baptized Marytjen, daughter of Frans De Lange and Marytjen Van Schaak, in the presence of Johannes Van Kleek and Aaltjen ter Bos, as witnesses. This is the first baptism recorded in the church book.

#### First Marriage.

The first marriage record bears date thirty years later. During all those years, the church was without a pastor, with the exception of the brief period (1731-3) covered by the pastorate of Dominie Van Schie. The records of both baptisms and marriages by him, during that brief period, have been lost. For the rest of the thirty years, the record of baptisms is nearly continuous. Mothers, being unable to travel, with their babes, through the forest to the minister at New Paltz or Kingston, waited for the minister to come from Kingston or New Paltz to Poughkeepsie, and, consequently, the baptisms took place at Poughkeepsie, and were recorded in the book of the church of Poughkeepsie. But, for the same years, there is no record of marriages in the book of the church of Poughkeepsie, and the presumption is, that those of the Poughkeepsie congregation who wished to be married, went for that purpose to the minister of some one of the neighboring churches, and that the marriages are recorded in the books of those churches.

The first record of marriage in the church book of Poughkeepsie is in the handwriting of the second pastor, Benjamin Meynema, and is as follows:

Register der getrouwde Perzonen na 3 afroepinge:

Ao. 1746, d. 31 January, zyn huwelyks geboden aangetekent van Petrus Freer jongman geboren in de Palts en Cornelia Oostrum jonge dogter geboren in Pakeepsie, en beyde woonagtig aldaar, en syn getrouwt de 25. Febr. 1746.

*Translation.*—Register of persons married after three publishments:

Anno 1746, January 31, were registered the marriage banns of Petrus Freer, bachelor, born in the Paltz, and Cornelia Oostrum, spinster, born in Poughkeepsie, and both there residing, and were married, February 25, 1746.

*First Receipt for Salary.*

Among the loose papers preserved are receipts for salary, in the handwriting of all the early pastors. One, in the handwriting of the first pastor, Cornelius Van Schie, is as follows:

Ik ondergeschreven bekenne uyt handen van de E. Kerkenraadt op Pakeepsie ontfangen te hebben voor de waarneming van myn dienst aldaar de somma van seventien ponden en tien schellingen Nieuw York gelt ter afbetaling van myn half jaar

## Miscellanea. 121

tractement t welk verschenen was de negende December, Anno seventien hondert twe en dertigh.

Pakeepsie, den 25, Jany, Anno 1732-3.
item 15 schell.
voor paarde voer.

CORN. VAN SCHIE,
V. D. M. ibidem.

*Translation.*—I, the underigned, acknowledge to have received from the hands of the Rev. Consistory of Poughkeepsie, for the performance of my ministry there, the sum of seventeen pounds and ten shillings, New York money, in payment of my half year's salary, which was due the ninth of December, Anno seventeen hundred and thirty-two.

Poughkeepsie, January 25, 1732-3.
item, 15 shillings for horse feed.

CORN. VAN SCHIE,
*Minister of the Word of God there.*

In the call which was accepted by Dominie Van Schie, the salary promised was seventy pounds a year, and three pounds additional for horse feed, one-half to be paid by the church of Poughkeepsie, and the other half by the church of Fishkill; and consequently the sums specified in the foregoing receipt were precisely those which were due from the church of Poughkeepsie for the half year.

### *Seats in the First Edifice.*

It has already been stated, that the seats in the first edifice for worship were assigned by the church masters, in August, 1723. The following is given as a fair specimen of the assignments:

Peter Palmetier—1 seat in No. 1 for himself, . . 36-0
 2 seats in No. 3 for his wife and daughter, . . 50-0
 1 seat in No. 8 for Michael Palmatier, . . . 30-0
 1 seat in No. 6 for Myndert Palmatier, . . . 30-0
 1 seat in No. 12 for Elizabeth Palmatier, . . 19-0

The prices are in guilders, each one being equal in value to a New York shilling. The highest price marked for a single seat is 36 guilders ($4.50), and the lowest price is 19 guilders ($2.37½).

From the extract given above, it is evident that the members of the family did not sit together; but were distributed to no less than five separate pews; and this seems to have been the case with the majority of families. It does not appear, however, from the record, that the men and women were separated, for there are a few cases in which a pew is assigned to a man and his family, and there are many cases in which seats in the same pew are assigned to both men and women of different families.

*Deed Conveying First Property.*

The following is a copy of the deed conveying the land on which the first edifice for worship was built:

To ALL CRISTIAN PEOPLE To whom these presents Shall or May Come Greeting Know Ye That I Jacobes Van Den Bogert of Dutches County in the Colonia of New York Yoman for and in Concederation of Divers good Causes and valuable Consederations by Me Recevid of Cap't Barendt Van Kleeck, Mr. Myndert Van Den Bogert Mr. Pieter fielee and Mr. Johannes Van Kleeck ALL yomen in the above said County the Recep't whereof I Do hierby acknowlidge And therewith fully satisfied and Contentid and thereof and of every paert And parcell thereof Do Exonerate aquitt and dischaerge the S$^d$ Barendt Van Kleeck Myndert Van Den Bogert pieter fielee and Johannes Van Kleeck there heirs Executors and Administrators for Ever by these presents HAVE giveing grantid bargained sould Alinenatid Convaied Confurmed and by these presents Do freely fully and absolutly give graent bargain Sell Alline Convey and Confurm unto the said Barendt Van Kleeck Myndert Van Den Bogert pieter fielee and Johannes Van Kleeck there heirs and assigns foreEver one Cartaine pies or Lott of ground Scituated Lyieng and being in pochkepseng in the afore said County, butted and Boundett Vz on the Nort Sid to the Rood that Runs to the Eastard to the forsaid Cap't Barendt Van Kleecks and on the west along the Rood that Runs to the Sout to Mr. Jonar La Roy's to the Sout and to the East to the Land of the Said Jacobes Van Den bogert it beieng a Corner Lott and in Lenght one hunderid and fifty foot and in breth one hunderid and fifty foot beieng a four squaer Lodt To HAVE AND TO HOULD the said grantid and bargained premoses with all the appurtenances and prevoleges and Commoditis to the same belongeng or in any wise aportaneng To them the said Barendt Van kleeck Myndert Van Den Bogert pieter fielce and Johannes Van Kleeck there heirs and assigns for Ever FOR THE PROPER And onely use benefitt and behoof of the Inhabatance and Naberhod of pochkepsen afore said to bild and maentaen a proper Mieteng hous to worship the one and onely Thriceonely God Acording to the Ruels and Methods as it is agried and Concludett by the Sinode National kept at Dordreght in the Year 1618 and 1619 and that in the Neder Dutch Lingoo and manner as it is now used by the Classes and Church of Amsterdam with the benefitt of the Mietenhous yaerd for a Bureall place of Christian Corps to the same belongeng with all the benefits and behoef for Ever and I the said Jacobes Van Den Bogert for mee my heirs exekutors and adm'rs do Covonent promes to and wid the said Barendt Van kleeck Myndert Van Den Bogert pieter fielce & Johannes van kleeck there heirs and assignes that before the ensealeng heir of I am the true soul and Lawfull owner of the above bargained and grantid premoses and am Lawfully seized and posesed of the same in my one proper Right As a good perfeckt and absolute estate of Enharetance and have In my Self good Right full pouer and Lawful autorety to graent bargain Sell Convey and Confurm the Said bargained and grantid premises in a manner as above Said and that the S$^d$ Barendt Van kleeck Myndert Van Den Bogert pieter fielee & Johannes Van kleeck there heirs and assignes Shall and may from time to time and at all times for Ever hier after for the use afore Said by vertue of these presents Lawfully peaceably and quiatly have hould use occupy possess and in Joy the said Demised and bargained premoses with the appurtenances free and Clier and freely and acquitted Exonerated and Dischaerge of and from all and allmanner of former gifts graents bargacins Seals Leases Mortgnages wills Entacils joynters Dowries Judgements Executions incumbrances Troubles whatso Ever and I the said Jacobes Van Den Bogert Do further bind my Self my heirs Exekutors and Admonestrators furmly by these presents to warrent and Defend the S$^d$ Barendt Van kleeck Myndert Van Den Bogert pieter fielee & Johannes Van kleeck there heirs and assignes in quiatt and peasable possession of all and Singular the S$^d$ granted premoses aginst all Lawful Claim of any parson or parsons by from or under mee IN WITTNESS whereof I the S$^d$ Jacobes Van Den Bogert have hier unto sett my hand and Seall this 26 Day of Desember in the year 1716.

Sined Selied and
Delivered In the
Presents of US
Barendt nukerck.
Matijs ven Stenbergh.

JACOBES VAN DEN BOGERT.
[SEAL.]

DUTCHIS COUNTY, May the 6 Annog Domney 1718.
Then appereth before me Leonard Lewis one of his Magistyes Gusteses of the Peace Mr. Jacobes Van Den Bogert and declareth this within Enstrument which he has Signed Sealled and Delivered to be his Volentary act and deed.

LEONARD LEWIS.

This Transport is Recorded In Dutchis County the 20th day of August Anno Dom. 1718 In Pages 1 and 2 at Pochkepsing by Henry Van Derburgh *Clark*.

## CHRONOLOGICAL CONSPECTUS.

| EVENTS. | PASTORS. |
|---|---|
| 1716. Organization. | |
| 1716. First Recorded Baptism | |
| 1716. Deed of Jacobus Van de Bogart. | |
| 1717. First edifice begun. | No Pastor |
| 1723. First edifice finished and seats assigned. | till 1731. |
| 1730. Union with Church of Fishkill. | |
| 1730. First call sent to Holland. | Cornelius Van Schie, 1731–3. |
| 1732. First Parsonage built. | |
| 1741. New roof and gallery for first edifice. | No Pastor, 1733–45. Benjamin Meynema, |
| 1746. First recorded marriage | 1745–56. Jacobus Van Nist, |
| 1760. Second edifice built. | 1758–61. Henricus Schoonmaker, 1763–74. |

| | |
|---|---|
| 1774. Union with Fishkill dissolved. | Isaac Rysdyck, 1765–72. (Two Pastors for seven years.) Stephen Van Voorhis, 1773–6. Solomon Froeligh, 1776–80. John H. Livingston, 1781–3. |
| 1789. Incorporation. | No Pastor. 1783–90. |
| 1791. Second Parsonage built. 1793. Seal adopted. 1793. Dutch preaching only every third Lord's day. | Andrew Gray, 1790–4. |
| 1794. Preaching all English. | Cornelius Brouwer, 1794–1808. |
| 1822. Election of Elders and Deacons by male members of Church. 1822. Third Edifice built. 1825. Sunday School first mentioned, but mentioned as previously existing. | Cornelius C. Cuyler, 1809–33. |
| 1835. D. R. Thompson, Superintendent of Sunday School. | Samuel A. Van Vranken, 1834–7. |
| 1844. Third Parsonage built. 1847. Second Reformed Church of Poughkeepsie formed. 1854. Third Edifice renovated. 1857. Third Edifice destroyed by fire. 1857. Fourth Edifice built. | Alexander M. Mann, 1838–57. |
| 1863. John H. Mathews, Superintendent of Sunday School. | George M. McEckron, 1858–67. |

1871. Election of officers by all the members of Church.   A. P. Van Gieson, 1867–.
1875. Henry S. Jewett, Superintendent of Sunday School.
1876. Milton A. Fowler, Superintendent of Sunday School.
1878. Spire taken down.
1887. Interior renovated.
1891. Election of officers by all members of Church of age of eighteen or over.

# PRESENT ORGANIZATION.

The present organization of the Church is as follows, viz:

## CONSISTORY.

*Pastor*—REV. A. P. VAN GIESON.

| *Elders.* | *Deacons.* |
|---|---|
| David C. Foster, | Charles D. Johnson, |
| Daniel R. Thompson, | Chester A. George, |
| Milton A. Fowler, | James M. Hadden, |
| Charles C. More, | George W. Polk, |
| Marvin O. Dutton, | Henry E. Losey, |
| John W. Pelton, | Charles R. Dickinson. |

*Clerk*, . . Milton A. Fowler.
*Treasurer*, . . John W. Pelton.
*Church Masters*, . { Charles D. Johnson, Chester A. George.
*Music Committee*, . { George W. Polk, Marvin O. Dutton.
*Finance Committee*, { Charles C. More, Henry E. Losey.

## SUNDAY SCHOOL.

*Superintendent*, . . . . Milton A. Fowler.
*Assistant Supt.*, . . Chester A. George.
*Secretary*, . . . . Leonard C. Miller.
*Librarian*, . . . . Charles Klady.
*Assistant Librarians*, { James E. Dickinson, William R. Vail.
*Manager of Primary Department*,
Mrs. Josephine Pardee.

*Present Organization.*

## YOUNG PEOPLE'S ALLIANCE.

*President,* . . . . . J. Elting Deyo.
*Vice-President,* . . . . Nettie Wilson.
*Secretary,* . . . . . . . Carrie E. Betz.
*Treasurer,* . . . . . . Edgar D. Van Nosdall.
Membership, 111.

## LADIES' SOCIETY.

*President,* . . . . . Mrs. M. O. Dutton.
*Vice-President,* . . Mrs. M. A. Fowler.
*Treasurer,* . . . Mrs. E. R. Williams.
*Secretary,* . Miss M. D. Van Gieson.

*Executive Committee.*

Mrs. Samuel H. Brown,   Mrs. Jane H. Mandeville,
Miss Nettie Farnum,     Mrs. B. W. Van Wyck,
Mrs. Samuel L. Dearin,  Mrs. Smith L. De Garmo,
Mrs. Warren S. Foster,  Mrs. C. D. Johnson.

*Home Mission Committee.*

Mrs. Samuel H. Brown,
Mrs. C. D. Johnson,
Mrs. Smith L. De Garmo.

## FOREIGN AND DOMESTIC MISSIONARY SOCIETY.

*President,* . . . . . Mrs. Samuel W. Buck.
*Vice-President,* . . Mrs. William A. Miles.
*Secretary,* . . . Mrs. Floy M. Johnston.
*Treasurer,* . . Mrs. J. H. Mandeville.
*Cor. Sec.,* . . Mrs. J. R. Reynolds.

www.ingramcontent.com/pod-product-compliance
Lightning Source LLC
Chambersburg PA
CBHW020111170426

**43199CB00009B/483**